PHOE³NIX

Mack Story

Bren Briggs

Copyright © 2016 Mack Story & Bren Briggs

Note: PHOENIX image on cover designed by Minuteman Press, Fayetteville, GA

All rights reserved.

ISBN-10: 153702650X
ISBN-13: 978-1537026503

DEDICATION

To those with the courage to move beyond their current
circumstances in order to transform themselves
into the person they were destined to be.

CONTENTS

	Introduction	1
1	Thought is the foundation of choice	5
2	Thoughts are based on values	8
3	Values on display	11
4	Choice is the foundation of vision	15
5	Choices create the future	18
6	A guy with a can do spirit	21
7	Vision is the foundation of hope	24
8	Vision provides direction	27
9	The rise of The Eden Project	30
10	Hope is the foundation of sacrifice	34
11	Hope is not a strategy	37
12	The ultimate sacrifice	40
13	Sacrifice is the foundation of discipline	43
14	Sacrifice demonstrates commitment	46
15	When you touch a life, you don't always feel it	49
16	Discipline is the foundation of growth	52
17	Discipline leverages sacrifice	55

18	The power to persevere	58
19	Growth is the foundation of change	61
20	Growth creates options	64
21	Staying positive through it all	67
22	Change is the foundation of success	70
23	Change releases potential	73
24	One more day	76
25	Success is the foundation of significance	80
26	Success creates momentum	83
27	Showdown in the sky	86
28	Significance is the foundation of legacy	89
29	Significance is not about you, but it starts with you	92
30	25 minutes that changed history	95

ACKNOWLEDGMENTS

We would like to thank those who have a desire to help others become the best version of themselves.

INTRODUCTION

"What distinguishes winners from losers is that winners concentrate at all times on what they can do, not what they can't do." ~ Bob Butera

Top Story Leadership and *The Eden Project* have collaborated to create this resource for you. It will be a core element of *The PHOE³NIX Project* serving as a source of motivation and inspiration to help you climb to the next level and beyond as you continue your mission. *The PHOE³NIX Project* is intended to help ENCOURAGE, ENGAGE, and EMPOWER you as you become more focused and intentional about moving from where you are to where you want to be.

In 2008, Mack Story co-founded *Top Story Leadership*, a Professional Leadership Development and Executive Coaching Consulting Firm, with his wife, Ria Story. Their motto is: POWERFUL LEADERSHIP – SIMPLIFIED. As of mid-2016, Mack and Ria have published 11 books, all related to personal growth and leadership development. They are both certified by leadership guru John C. Maxwell to speak and train on many of his best-selling books. Mack and Ria worked with John as part of the *Transformation Begins with Me* cultural transformation initiative in Guatemala in 2013 where more than 20,000 Guatemalan leaders were trained. They have supported multi-billion dollar organizations such as Chick-fil-A, Koch Industries, Danaher – Pall, Brose, and others.

Mack's personal growth journey began in 1987 when he joined the United States Marine Corps as an 0311 Infantryman. He has an extensive background in manufacturing with over 20 years focusing on process improvement (Lean). As an external consultant, he has led leaders and their cross-functional teams through over 11,000 hours of process improvement, change, and cultural transformation. He has a passion for helping people become more than they think they can be. His mission is to help you unleash your potential.

Bren Briggs is a retired Army officer with 28 years of service to his country. He is a Lean Six Sigma Master Black Belt and has an MA in Leadership. Bren has worked within the DoD, large for-profit companies, and has lead enterprise level transformation efforts saving the tax payers millions of dollars. He has coached and mentored many top leaders across the Army. With multiple deployments of his own, Bren has spent the last ten years working with other warriors and their families through the difficulties associated with long separation and injuries. Through this, he developed *The Eden Project* concept. Bren is the founder of *The Eden Project* which is made up of warriors and supporters dedicated to the healing process for those who have served our country.

The Eden Project is a warrior centric organization, fully immersed in each community that brings a holistic, multi-disciplinary approach to caring for warriors and their families. They believe the foundation of wellbeing and path to healing starts in the home with a strong support system. Therefore, the primary emphasis and core focus is the family and support network for the warrior. They use a comprehensive individualized support plan specifically designed for each warrior and his or her support network.

In addition, *The Eden Project* also focuses on two other areas: world class medical care with a focus on TBI and PTSD and professional career development training. Lastly, they offer a full range of training to prepare for an effective and efficient transition from a military career to a civilian one.

As you begin your journey through this material, you must understand the book is based on the *10 Foundational Elements of Transformation.* Each "layer" of the foundation is supported by those layers that come before it. The book is divided into 10 sections, one for each of the foundational layers of transformation.

In each section, Mack's leadership principles are combined with Bren's extensive military experience. The first two chapters of each section were written by Mack and are intended to introduce and teach you fundamental principles. The third chapter in each section was written by Bren and supports the previous two chapters.

This material will build upon itself as you make your way through it. It will be much more meaningful if read at least two times because the layers above add meaning to the layers below. Reflection and re-reading will greatly enhance your understanding.

Make this book a tool and a resource. Mark it up. Fold the pages. Highlight and underline key points. However, DON'T GIVE IT AWAY. If you think someone else will get value from it, invest in them and purchase one for them as a gift, so they can also mark it up and use it as a resource of their own.

Your ability to effectively move from where you are to where you want to be in any area of your life will be determined by your ability to transform your thinking relative to that area of your life. When it comes to true transformation, if you don't go within, you will go without. You are the key to your own success.

"If you truly want to initiate a change that will redirect your life and unleash your potential, focus on transforming yourself." ~ Mack Story

SECTION 1

THOUGHT IS THE FOUNDATION OF CHOICE

1

THOUGHT IS THE FOUNDATION OF CHOICE

WHAT YOU THINK DETERMINES WHAT YOU DO

"The outer world of circumstance shapes itself to the inner world of thought." ~ James Allen

If you already knew what you needed to know, you would already be where you want to go. Until you change what you think, you will not change what you do.

Your conscious thoughts are real but only in y*our* mind. Your thoughts will lead to other private thoughts and subconscious feelings or emotions. Once you act on your thoughts and feelings, they are translated to the world as choices when they begin to shape your life.

You first make your choices. Then, your choices make you.

The Choice Formula:
Thought + Emotion + Action = Choice

Thought – something we are consciously aware of in our mind
Emotion – something we subconsciously feel based on our thoughts
Action – something we do based on our thoughts and emotions

Your choices flow from your thoughts. The quality of the choices depends on the quality of the thoughts. There is no conscious choice without conscious thought.

Think of what your home looks like or think of your favorite car. Not only can you choose your thoughts, but as you just experienced in this simple exercise, it is very easy for others to influence your thoughts. This is where our real problems start. Far too often, we accept bad influence instead of rejecting it and using our own reasoning to positively influence our thoughts.

James Allen in his book, *As a Man Thinketh*, wrote, *"Our mind may be likened to a garden, which may be intelligently cultivated or allowed to run wild; but whether cultivated or neglected, it must, and will, bring forth. If no useful seeds are put into it, then an abundance of useless weed-seeds will fall therein, and will continue to produce their kind."*

Our mind can be prepared to produce great thoughts and choices just as a freshly plowed field is made ready to produce a great crop. Our mind can also be left undeveloped or underdeveloped to produce whatever thoughts it may without any intentional development. But make no mistake, our mind will produce thoughts. Thoughts and choices will flow from our mind whether good or bad, beneficial or harmful. *Sought or not, there will be thought.* Thoughts will sprout from our mind as plants sprout from the earth. Abundantly.

When you garden, you are responsible for planting seeds capable of producing a great crop. Likewise, you are responsible for developing your mind to produce great thoughts and choices beneficial to you and others. Thoughts that will lead you to where you want to be.

You can take another step and work the garden continuously by watering, weeding, and fertilizing to ensure and enhance the quality of the crop. You can go farther in the development of your mind by associating with people who want to help you by choosing to remove bad habits and bad people from your life, by intentionally studying positive people, by reading positive books, and by making positive choices.

One very powerful life and death choice is self-talk, *thoughts* you have about yourself and others. Self-talk is far more destructive than what others say to you or about you. Why? Because you are always listening to yourself.

People take their lives every day because of their own self-talk, not what others are saying. Sometimes they are not talking to others at all. Their own thoughts have brought them to the point of feeling worthless, helpless, and most often, hopeless. They have convinced themselves there is no reason to continue living.

These people no longer have hope and have given up. When you don't have hope, you must get it from others. You must connect with positive people, be with them, and talk with them. You must borrow their belief in you. They can and will lift you up. If the people you are around don't lift you up, you are around the wrong people. The right people will *always* give you hope and lift you up.

There are endless examples of self-talk (thought) being detrimental to our well-being. You can choose your thoughts and change your thoughts. When you do, you change your habits, your circumstances, and your life.

"We imagine that thought can be kept secret, but it cannot; it rapidly crystallizes into habit, and habit solidifies into circumstance." ~ James Allen

2

THOUGHTS ARE BASED ON VALUES

HIGH IMPACT VALUES LEAD TO HIGH IMPACT THOUGHTS

*"I cannot teach anybody anything,
I can only make them think." ~ Socrates*

Ultimately, you choose your results when you choose your values. *Your values are the foundation for your results.*

Your values influence your thoughts, which influence your feelings, which influence your actions, which *determine* your results. Dramatically different values will always lead to dramatically different results.

V. Gilbert Beers had this to say about values, *"A person of integrity is one who has established a system of values against which all of life is judged."*

Everyone has values. They can be good or bad. You categorize them as good or bad by asking, "Are my values in alignment with natural laws and principles?" Natural laws and principles are timeless. Every human understands them regardless of age, race, religion, gender, etc. Fairness is a great example. No one ever taught you the thousands of ways you can be treated unfairly. However, you know when it happens because you *feel* it.

You came fully loaded with the innate ability to understand right and wrong. And, you also came fully loaded with free will, the ability to choose to adhere to natural laws and principles or to go completely against them. You have an internal "map" with street lights along the path you should take, but you also have the awareness and ability to see and travel the dimly lit and dark paths you should avoid.

Do you *value* accepting responsibility or transferring responsibility? When you look through the window and blame others, you are transferring responsibility. Statements like "You make me so mad!" are said by those who choose to blame and transfer responsibility. When you look in the mirror to find the solution to your problems, you are accepting responsibility. Statements like "How was this my fault?" and "What could I have done differently?" are said by those who choose to reflect on and accept responsibility for the situation.

Your values are the foundation upon which you base your thoughts. My book, *10 Values of High Impact Leaders,* details 10 key values everyone should work to master because those values will have a tremendous impact on one's ability to positively influence others. The more influence you have, the more options you will have. Since influence is very dynamic, the more values you have been able to internalize and utilize synergistically together, the more effective you will be and the more influence you will have. So, where do you start?

There is a story of a tourist who paused for a rest in a small town in the mountains. He went over to an old man sitting on a bench in front of the only store in town and inquired, "Friend, can you tell me something this town is noted for?"

"Well," replied the old man, "I don't rightly know except it's the starting point to the world. You can start here and go anywhere you want."

That's a great little story. We are all at *the starting point to the world*. We can *start where we are and go anywhere*. We can expand our influence 360° in all directions by simply starting in the center and expanding ourselves.

Consider the illustration below. Imagine you are standing in the center. You can make a high impact. However, it will not happen by accident. You *must* become *intentional*. You must *live with purpose* while *focusing on your performance* as you *unleash your potential*.

Why we do what we do is about our *purpose*. *How* we do what we do is about our *performance*. *What* we do will unleash our *potential*. Where these three components overlap, you will achieve a **HIGH IMPACT**.

"The values that form the basis for your True North are derived from your beliefs and convictions. In defining your values, you must decide what is most important in your life. Is it maintaining your integrity, making a difference, helping other people, or devoting yourself to family? There is no one right set of values. Only you can decide the question of your values." ~ Bill George

3

VALUES ON DISPLAY

WHO YOU ARE ON THE INSIDE IS WHAT OTHERS EXPERIENCE ON THE OUTSIDE

"It's the unconquerable soul of man, not the nature of the weapon he uses, that insures victory."
~ Gen. George S. Patton

Private First Class (PFC) Sasser was a young man who was drafted into service during the Vietnam War. Although he spent a mere 51 days in country, the decisions he made and actions he took will live on forever.

In early January 1968, PFC Sasser was assigned to US Army, Headquarters Company, 3d Battalion, 60th Infantry, 9th Infantry Division with action in and around Ding Tuong Province, Republic of Vietnam. He did not set out to be a hero, and I am sure he did not plan to do what he did that January day in 1968. But, his choices led to actions that saved the lives of over half a dozen Soldiers. His company was making an air assault when suddenly it came under heavy small arms, machine gun, and rocket fire from well-fortified enemy positions on three sides of the landing zone. PFC Sasser was serving as a medical corpsman with Company A, 3d Battalion, on a reconnaissance in force operation.

Within a few minutes, over 30 casualties were sustained in his unit. Without hesitation, PFC Sasser ran across an open rice paddy through a hail of fire to assist the wounded. After helping one man to safety, PFC Sasser was painfully wounded in the left shoulder by fragments of a rocket propelled grenade. Refusing medical attention for himself, he ran through another barrage of rocket and automatic weapons fire to aid casualties of the initial attack. After giving them urgently needed treatment, he continued to search for other wounded Soldiers.

PFC Sasser received two additional wounds to his legs. He quickly immobilized his legs and dragged himself through the mud toward another Soldier about 100 meters away. Although he was in a tremendous amount of pain and faint from loss of blood, PFC Sasser reached the other Soldier, rendered aid, and proceeded on to encourage another group of Soldiers. He encouraged this other group of Soldiers to crawl 200 meters to reach a position which provided more cover and safety. Injured himself, PFC Sasser continued to provide aide for the other Soldiers for an additional five hours until they were evacuated.

PFC Sasser's extraordinary heroism that day earned him the country's highest honor, the Congressional Medal of Honor. Additionally, he also received a Purple Heart for his injuries and a Combat Action Badge.

I am sure this humble Soldier would tell you he did not consciously plan the actions he undertook that day in 1968. However, he was a man of value and positive thought. Ultimately, he chose his values. And through those values, his thoughts and actions determined the choices he made that day. As a result, half a dozen men have their lives.

PFC Sasser, after recovering from his own injuries and finishing his military commitment, attended college and studied chemistry. Later, he worked for the Department of Veterans Affairs. He currently lives in Texas.

*"Professionalism has a flavor;
do all you can to improve the taste."
~ Congressional Medal of Honor recipient,
USMC Col. Wesley Fox*

SECTION 2

CHOICE IS THE FOUNDATION OF VISION

4

CHOICE IS THE FOUNDATION OF VISION

IF YOU DON'T KNOW WHERE YOU'RE GOING, YOU WILL END UP SOMEWHERE ELSE

"Destiny is not a matter of chance, but a matter of choice. It is not a thing to be waited for but is a thing to be achieved." ~ William Jennings Bryan

There is no conscious action without conscious thought. You can turn your potential into your reality. The quality of your *choices* depends on the quality of your thoughts. When is the last time you spent 10 minutes per day for 90 consecutive days thinking about where you want to be and how you're going to get there? Doing so is simply a *choice* you can make.

Most people haven't spent even one day thinking intentionally for 10 minutes about where they want to be and how they are going to get there. Far too many people get trapped in a never ending cycle of doing the same thing day in and day out while hoping, wishing, and praying for different results. This makes absolutely no sense when you *actually* think about it. But, most people *don't* think about it.

You are responsible for *choosing* to move yourself forward. Until you *choose* to realize this simple fact, you will be at the mercy of society. And, society doesn't have a lot planned for you. Once you make the *choice* to become responsible you have positioned yourself to make some amazing things happen.

As Dee Ann Turner stated so simply, *"Wise choices in the beginning provide a better chance of success in the end."* When you make the *choice* to respond to everything based on internalized values that are timeless, tested, and have been proven across generations, you are prepared to launch yourself to the next level and beyond.

When it comes to creating a compelling vision for yourself, you must intentionally tap into your passion and purpose to begin to think of what could be. Too many people chase money instead of happiness. As a result, they get neither. You will be the happiest when you're earning a living doing something you are passionate about and that interests you. Odds are, you will also earn more money over a lifetime doing it. And if you don't, you won't care because you'll be happy simply doing what you love.

Developing a vision, big or small, is a *choice*. We must think on purpose about our purpose. Most people are far removed from their purpose. When asked what their purpose is, most don't have an answer. However, the most common answer is, "I don't know." Or, "I've never really thought about it."

If you're serious about creating a life worth living, it's time to *choose* to think about your purpose. Once you know who you are and who you want to become and where you are and where you want to be, you can begin your transformation. Transformation is a choice that only responsible people can and will make.

Transformation turns vision into reality. You must intentionally *choose* to dream of what is possible. You must *choose* to let your imagination run wild. Who do you want to become? What do you want to do? Where do you want to go? When do you want to go? Don't ask, "Can I do it?" Ask, "Is it possible?" Think, "How can I make it happen?" and "When can I make it happen?" Then, follow up with the most important question of all, "What's stopping me from making it happen?"

When you ask these questions, don't look out the window for excuses. An effective vision taps into your strengths not your weaknesses. Look into the mirror, *choose* to be responsible, and find a way. You are exactly where you're supposed to be based on every choice you've made leading up to this moment.

Will things outside of your control happen to you? Absolutely…until the day you die. Those things are important and will influence you along your journey. However, there's something much more important than what happens to you.

The most important thing is your response to what happens to you. You don't always get to choose what happens to you. But, you will *always* get to *choose* your response to what happens to you. Your response will determine much, but not all, of what happens to you in the future.

Regardless of what has happened to you or what will happen to you in the future, the *choices* you make daily will *always* shape your future. When you *choose* to intentionally create a vision for your future, you're aligned to make the *choices* that will create that future. Things will happen outside of your control. When they do, you simply regroup, reevaluate the situation, look forward, make the necessary adjustments, and continue creating your future.

> *"A man's environment is a merciless mirror of him as a human being." ~ Earl Nightingale*

5

CHOICES CREATE THE FUTURE

WHAT WE CHOOSE TO DO TODAY WILL DETERMINE WHAT WE GET TO DO TOMORROW

"Show me someone who is humble enough to accept and take responsibility for his or her circumstances and courageous enough to take whatever initiative is necessary to creatively work his or her way through or around these challenges, and I'll show you the supreme power of choice." ~ Dr. Stephen R. Covey

When you *choose* to accept responsibility for your future, you will be able to define your future.

Apply what's on these pages, and you'll be amazed at the future you will create. A future you can't begin to imagine now. There are opportunities for you right now that you can't see. You must start preparing for those opportunities without knowing what they are. You must trust they are there and begin moving toward them.

It's much like taking a trip in a car at night. You can't see very much in the dark. If you want to see ahead in the dark, you must first turn on the lights. Then, if you want to see even farther ahead, you must start moving slowly in the direction you think you want to go. As you move, you will begin to see the previously unseen.

Your growth toward a better and preferred future is exactly the same. You're holding in your hand a way forward, if you'll turn the light on (take responsibility) and start moving forward (growth) toward your vision. As Dr. Henry Cloud says, *"If you have already been trying hard, maybe trying harder is not the way. Try different."*

If you don't choose to create your future, the cumulative choices of society will determine your future. You can choose to navigate your way to your destination, or you can refuse to navigate your way to your destination. If you refuse to navigate your way forward, it's like being adrift in the ocean. There's no telling where you'll end up or when you'll get there. In other words, you will be helpless and hopeless.

Unfortunately, that's exactly how many people live their lives. They are where they are because that's where they ended up. By not choosing to be someplace else, they chose to be there. By not choosing to navigate their way forward, they simply drifted into a career or job, and maybe, into a bad relationship. Instead of intentionally creating their future, they accidentally created their future.

Too often, people who are searching in life find what they will settle for and stop looking for what they were searching for. As John G. Miller remarked, *"There's nothing you have to do. We all have the power to make a decision that will direct us to a new destination. Each of us can make a choice that will change our life."*

The future is in you now. Think about that for a moment. Your future really is in you now. That's not just a play on words. It's the truth. Your future is defined and refined by the *choices* you make every day. Make a bad *choice*, and you get a less desirable future. Make a good *choice*, and you get a more desirable future. You can easily see you are very much in control of creating your future. You don't have to settle. It's your choice.

You can't predict your future, but *you can create your future*. This is powerful and profound if you have never taken the time to slow down and truly think it out. The thousands of *choices* we make every day of our life, not only shape our life, but they also create our future.

Remember, with only a few exceptions, you're exactly where you're supposed to be based on all of the *choices* you have made leading up to this moment. If you were supposed to be someplace else, you would already be there. You must own the results your *choices* have produced. James Allen said it best, *"We are anxious to improve our circumstances but unwilling to improve ourselves. We therefore remain bound."*

Until you own that you're responsible, you're being irresponsible. That's why those blaming others for their circumstances can't improve their circumstances.

The thought process of blaming someone else for your circumstances has a zero chance of making anything in your life better. Many people wake up and live out this model from start to finish every day.

Why? Because when we blame others, we don't have to do anything. We truly believe someone else is responsible, and think they should do everything. But, when we take the blame, we are 100% responsible. Now, *we* must do everything. Most people take the easy way out and blame others for their circumstances.

Don't be fearful. Be hopeful. It's a choice.

"May your choices reflect your hopes, not your fears."
~ Nelson Mandela

6

A GUY WITH A CAN DO SPIRIT

ACTIONS DETERMINE RESULTS

"A good plan, violently executed now, is better than a perfect plan next week." ~ Gen. George S. Patton

Kyle Carpenter is currently in school in South Carolina where he is pursuing a degree in International Studies. He is also helping raise money and awareness for the Fisher House Foundation. This organization provides free and low-cost housing to veterans and families receiving treatment at military hospitals.

Kyle has been described as a guy with a can do spirit. It's out of this spirit that Lance Corporal Carpenter was honored with a Congressional Medal of Honor due to his heroism.

Kyle enlisted in the Marines in 2009 and was assigned to 2nd Battalion 9th Marines stationed at Camp Lejeune North Carolina. Shortly after his assignment to 2/9, his unit was sent to Afghanistan in support of Operation Enduring Freedom.

While there, he was an Automatic Rifleman with Fox Company in the Helmand Province. Lance Corporal Carpenter was a member of a platoon-sized coalition force comprised of two reinforced Marine rifle squads partnered with an Afghan National Army squad. The platoon had established Patrol Base Dakota two days earlier in a small village in the Marjah District in order to disrupt enemy activity and provide security for the local

Afghan population.

Lance Corporal Carpenter and a fellow Marine were manning a rooftop security position on the perimeter of Patrol Base Dakota when the enemy initiated a daylight attack with hand grenades, one of which landed inside their sandbagged position. Without hesitation and with complete disregard for his own safety, Lance Corporal Carpenter moved toward the grenade in an attempt to shield his fellow Marine from the deadly blast. When the grenade detonated, his body absorbed the brunt of the blast, severely wounding him, but saving the life of his fellow Marine. By his undaunted courage, bold fighting spirit, and unwavering devotion to duty in the face of almost certain death, Lance Corporal Carpenter reflected great credit upon himself and upheld the highest tradition of the Marine Corps.

Much of this story was taken directly from his Congressional Medal of Honor citation that speaks of his actions and quick thinking. People who know Kyle and speak of him also talk about his "can do" spirit and positive outlook. Carpenter lost his right eye and most of his teeth. His jaw and right arm were shattered. He has undergone over 30 surgeries and requires ongoing treatment. He is an inspiration to all who know him.

Lance Corporal Carpenter made a choice that day in Afghanistan, he chose to save his friend's life, and in doing so put his own life at risk. That single act, that instant decision, changed his life and the life of Lance Corporal Nick Eufrazio forever. He did not get to choose what happened to him, but he did choose his response and reaction. Every day, his choices shape his future and those around him.

"Luck favors those in motion." ~ *Gen. George S. Patton*

SECTION 3

VISION IS THE FOUNDATION OF HOPE

7

VISION IS THE FOUNDATION OF HOPE

WHAT WE CHOOSE TO IMAGINE MAKES US FEEL FEARFUL OR HOPEFUL

"There are three requirements for humans to act: 1) dissatisfaction with the present state of affairs, 2) a vision of a better state, and 3) belief that we can reach that better state. When just one of the requirements is missing, people will not act." ~ Ludwig von Mises

Several years ago, I discovered a rather odd but impactful story illustrating how vision can create hope. An experiment was performed with laboratory rats to measure their motivation to survive under different circumstances.

Scientists would drop a rat into a jar of water that had been placed in total darkness (no vision) and time how long the animal would continue swimming before it gave up (lost hope) and allowed itself to drown. The scientists discovered the rats would usually survive approximately three minutes in the dark without hope.

Next, the scientists dropped other rats individually into the same type of jar, but instead of placing them in total darkness, they allowed a ray of light (hope) to shine in.

Under those circumstances, the rat kept swimming for 36 hours with the ray of light (hope). That's 720 times longer than those trying to survive in the dark without hope!

Because the rats could see (vision), they continued to have hope. If this is true for a rat, imagine the amount of hope a strong and powerful personal vision will provide you. You are much more capable of imagining and reasoning yourself into a brighter future, one filled with light instead of darkness.

Once you have a clearly defined vision, you must again ask yourself, "Is it possible my vision can become my reality?" You may not be able to tell yourself with integrity you can do it. If not, don't lie to yourself. However, don't concern yourself with trying to decide if you can or can't do it. That's not important.

What is important is your belief that *it is possible*. Knowing it's possible will provide you with the hope you need to turn your vision into your reality.

You should also seek reinforcement from those who believe in you and your mission. Others who believe in you will also reinforce your belief that your vision is possible. Look for those who will support you and avoid those who won't.

Most often, people you don't know can help you the most. How can someone you don't know help you the most? Because they have written books to help people just like you.

You're reading a book right now, most likely written by someone you don't know, who wants to help you move forward. Someone who believes in you and your vision. Reading books written by people who have done what you want to do or by people who are doing what you want to do, allows you to get into some of the greatest minds with the most valuable insight.

Whatever you do, don't make the common mistake of asking your friends and relatives to validate your vision. Unless they have done what you want to do or are doing what you want to do, they are not likely to provide meaningful support. Instead, they will usually question your ability, provide plenty of reasons it can't or won't happen, and place doubt in your mind.

These people are not necessarily bad people. They simply haven't been where you've been and don't want to go where you're going. If you decide to climb to the top of Mt. Everest, you will obviously want to seek support, guidance, and direction from someone who has already been to the top (a tour guide). You will not want to seek support, guidance, and direction from someone who has only booked trips for people who want to climb to the top (a travel agent). This simple principle applies in all areas related to turning your vision into reality.

Viktor Frankl made this wise observation, *"Everyone has his own specific vocation or mission in life. Everyone must carry out a concrete assignment that demands fulfillment. Therein he cannot be replaced, nor can his life be repeated. Thus everyone's task is as unique as his specific opportunity to implement it."* You are unique. Your vision is unique. Some may not understand. That's okay. Make it happen anyway.

Without hope, your vision will fade into darkness just as it did with the rats. But with hope, your vision remains clear, giving you a reason to "keep swimming." You must maintain hope that your vision will become your reality.

Knowing it is possible will give you hope. Having faith in your vision will give you hope. Having people believe in you and your vision will give you hope. Knowing others have done what you want to do will give you hope.

"Cherish your vision and your dreams as they are the children of your soul, the blueprints of your ultimate achievements." ~ Napoleon Hill

8

VISION PROVIDES DIRECTION

KNOWING WHERE WE'RE GOING ALLOWS US TO CHART THE COURSE

"Clarity of vision will compensate for uncertainty in planning. If you are unclear about the destination of the journey, even the most sophisticated, well-thought-through strategy is useless. Pencil in your plans. Etch the vision in stone." ~ Andy Stanley

When your vision flows from your passion and purpose, you will find clarity and will become a highly effective and highly influential individual. You will begin to live a much more fulfilling and rewarding life. You will live a life most people will never experience, but many will dream about.

In order to fully leverage your passion to increase your influence, you must use it to find, reveal, and refine your *why* – your purpose. You must follow your passion to find your purpose. Discovering your purpose doesn't happen accidentally as you go through life. It happens intentionally as you grow through life. Finding your purpose sounds simple, but it's not. It requires a lot of discipline, stretching, risk taking, determination, and searching without settling.

Unfortunately, many people will go to their grave never discovering their *why*. Instead, they will choose to settle for mediocrity instead of greatness. Why would anyone settle for mediocrity when they could become exceptional? It's simple. Very little effort is required to be mediocre. However, to become exceptional, an extraordinary and continuous effort will be required. It takes a lot of work to continually grow and develop yourself, but it's worth it.

When you align your purpose with your vision you know you're heading in the right direction. A vision without a purpose is like having a map but no idea where you want to go. If you don't know where you want to go, a map will not do you any good at all. As a matter of fact, if you don't know where you're going, you don't even need a map.

This simple illustration explains why most people haven't defined a detailed vision for themselves. They don't know where they're going. They haven't fully accepted responsibility for developing their own personal vision. If they don't know where they're going and don't care where they're going, why do they need to see (create a vison for themselves)? They don't. They can simply wander through life while waiting to die. It sounds harsh. But, it's the choice many people make consciously or unconsciously.

Many people are not on a mission. They are not on a journey. They have no vision. They are wandering aimlessly through life waiting on something good to happen, waiting on life to give them a break, waiting to retire, and ultimately, waiting to die. That is not living. That is loafing.

William Barclay made a powerful statement when he said, *"There are two great days in a person's life – the day you are born and the day you discover why."* Everyone experiences the first day – the day we are born. It's hard to miss that one. However, very few experience the second day. Very few of us ever discover *why* we were born. This book will challenge you to discover *your* why. Or, if you're already well on your way to discovering your why, it will help you *leverage* your why.

No matter your passion and purpose, you must be able to influence people in order to add value to them and be valued by them. You must be able to influence them to voluntarily follow you. You must define and refine your vision in order to get closer to living the life you want instead of living the one you've been given. However, your ability to influence other people will determine where you're able to go and when you're able to go.

Everything in your life will rise and fall based on the amount of influence you're able to create with others. Your vision will help you identify who you need to influence. Your values, character, and competency will determine if you're actually able to influence them. Your vision will help you identify what you need to learn in order to be able to influence others along your journey.

Your vision will also help you discover who you need to become on the inside in order to influence the right people on the outside. Your vision will serve as your roadmap for growth.

The most important thing your vision will reveal is who you need to become and what you need to know. When it comes to vision, your character will take you most of the way. And, your competency will take you the rest of the way.

Many people don't want to create a vision for their life because they already know they are unwilling to put in the work. Without action, your vision will be just a dream.

> *"Vision is not enough. It must be combined with venture. It is not enough to stare up the steps; we must step up the stairs." ~ Vaclav Havel*

9

THE RISE OF THE EDEN PROJECT

HELPING OTHERS OVERCOME ADVERSITY

"No matter how significant or life-changing your greatest hit or miss might be, neither even begins to define all of who you are. Each of us is a product of all our experiences and all our interactions with other people." ~ Gen. Colin Powell

In 2006, during a training event while I (Bren Briggs) was deployed, I was injured. At the time, I knew I was hurt but didn't fully comprehend the extent of my injuries.

There was a searing pain on the right side of my face. Instinctively, I raised both hands and put my dislocated jaw back in place. Over the next three weeks, I would wake up at night with my jaw locked open and dislocated. Finally, I could no longer endure the pain, and I agreed to be redeployed home. Once at home, I began a seven-year journey of six reconstructive surgeries and trips every month to rehabilitation, therapy, and medical appointments, all of which I did alone.

It was during these appointments, times on the road traveling to and from the doctors' offices, hospital admissions, and countless hours in the waiting rooms that I was blessed to talk with other wounded warriors. Many of their stories were the same. All were proud to serve their country. Most would do it again even knowing the end result. And, a few had actually taken their situation and were making something good out of it.

I loved their positive attitude, mindset, and view on life. I too felt there was a reason for what I was going through and knew everything had a purpose. I was not sure what it was, but I continued to talk with others during their trials and did my best to keep their spirits up and motivate them whenever possible.

I intentionally sought out purpose and meaning for my circumstances. I was not bitter. I did not blame anyone, but I took action every day to develop a vision. A theme developed after a few years: Most of the people I met during this time were having problems with their marriages, with their health, and definitely with their thought processes. There was no way they could focus on their future while they were having so many problems with their present.

That's when my vision for the future started to appear. Honestly, it was dim at first. But over time, it grew brighter and brighter until it was all I could think about.

I knew I was here to help others avoid the problems I and many others were having at home. There seemed to be agencies that wanted to help with finding jobs, finding homes, writing resumes, going on fun excursions, and meeting some of the higher level needs. But, the lower level, basic needs were not being addressed. Therefore, the primary foundation was unstable. As a result, their lives, *our lives*, were in a constant state of imbalance. That is where my vision started.

My burning passion to help others sparked *The Eden Project*. The first few years, I was only able to talk with warriors and listen to their stories. I let them know they were not alone. I would be there, along with others who shared the vision, to provide a positive outlook for their current circumstance.

Often, we just need to know there is someone who actually cares enough to listen. We don't always need a lot of medication or long term therapy, although both are required in some situations. Some of us simply need to be validated and respected, and at times, to be provided with a reset button for our lives.

My passion to help others overcome adversity led to my vision. Now, my vision has become *our* reality. The vision is simple: Provide a world class, community-based program to help warriors and their families restore their marriage, rebuild their bodies, rejuvenate their minds, and create their futures. *The Eden Project* has helped scores of warriors and their families. We will continue to do so because we are intentionally focused on our passion which continues to refine our vision.

Everyone has the same potential inside of them. It's a matter of taking the time to look for it, identify it, and achieve it.

"The goal of a leader is to give no orders. Leaders are to provide direction and intent and allow others to figure out what to do and how to get there."
~ Capt. L. David Marquet

SECTION 4

HOPE IS THE FOUNDATION OF SACRIFICE

10

HOPE IS THE FOUNDATION OF SACRIFICE

WHEN THERE IS HOPE FOR THE FUTURE, THERE IS MEANING IN THE SACRIFICE

"There are no hopeless situations; there are only men and women who have grown hopeless about them."
~ Marshal Ferdinand Foch

Without hope, there will be no sacrifice. When you can see the potential for a better future and you believe it is possible, you develop hope. When there's hope for a better future, you are more likely to pay a price (sacrifice) to turn that preferred future into your reality.

Vision provides hope, and hope provides a reason to make sacrifices. For example, you may be able to see (vision) how a college degree will help you get a job in a field that interests you. The vision of getting the degree and being paid to do what you *want to do* instead of continuing to do what you *have to do* gives you hope for a better future.

Because you have hope for a better future, you will be more likely to sacrifice your resources, such as time, money, and activities, to do what is required to earn the degree you *feel* you need. However, if you don't *feel* having the degree will help, there will be no hope and no sacrifice. Without the sacrifice, you will not get the degree or, most likely, the job. Hope is a feeling.

Michael Hyatt got it right when he said, *"You can either accept reality as it is or create it as you wish it to be."* Those without hope simply accept reality as it is. Those with hope are positioned to create it as they wish it to be.

Without hope, you will be at the mercy of society. You will get what others want you to have when they want you to have it. Life does not have to be that way. As long as you are able to make choices, you will be able to change your circumstances. However, very little will change without hope for a better future.

Hope can inspire you from within to make the necessary sacrifices. When you have hope, you believe things will be better. When you consider your vision, you look at where you are and compare it to where you want to be. You don't hope for things to get worse. You hope for things to get better.

If you believe strongly enough in yourself and your vision (hope), you will have the strength and desire to make the many sacrifices needed to transform your vision into your reality. Hope allows you to look in the mirror, accept responsibility, and ask, "What can I do?" "What should I do?" And, "When should I do it?"

If you don't believe strongly enough in yourself and your vision (hopeless), you will not have the strength or desire to make the many sacrifices needed to transform your vision into your reality. Instead of hoping and sacrificing, you begin to wish and wonder. Those wishing and wondering tend to transfer responsibility, look out the window, and say, "I wish things were better." and "I wonder if things will ever change."

To move closer to your vision, you must first become more hopeful about the possibilities that lie ahead. You may have been through a lot. You may have already overcome a lot. But to move forward, regardless of who you are and where you are, you must continue to have hope for a better future. When you stop having hope, you will stop moving forward.

Sacrifice is giving up something of lesser value now for something of greater value later. Having the vision and foresight to see the greater value is not enough. You must act on that vision. When you give up something, you feel the loss immediately. However, you may not realize the gain until days, weeks, months, or even years later.

Hope is powerful and will help inspire you to make the tough choices. If you can't generate hope from within, from your thoughts or from your faith, there's only one other place to get it, from other people who believe in you. We've all had someone believe in us when we haven't believed in ourselves. That belief from the outside can work miracles on the inside.

If you find yourself hopeless, you must choose to borrow hope from the outside until you develop it on the inside. There are no excuses because we all have the freedom to choose our response in any circumstance. As James Allen stated so well, *"Circumstance does not make the man; it reveals him to himself."*

Do you need hope? Try talking to a friend or family member. Too often, people will say, "But, I don't have anyone to talk to." That's an *excuse* to remain hopeless, not a *reason* to remain hopeless. Read a book. Books have given many people hope. Books have transformed many lives. Books have even saved lives. If you want to be hopeful, you can be. It's a choice. If you want to be hopeless, you can be. That's also a choice.

"Extraordinary people survive under the most terrible circumstances and then become more extraordinary because of it." ~ Robertson Davies

11

HOPE IS NOT A STRATEGY

HOPE HAS THE POWER TO LAUNCH YOU, BUT HOPE CANNOT DELIVER YOU

"It really is amazing what happens when you recognize the importance of the opportunities ahead of you, accept responsibility for your future, and take positive action." ~ Michael F. Sciortino, Sr.

Hope is not a strategy. However, hope is necessary to develop a strategy. Why? Without hope, you won't be inspired to develop a strategy. Without hope, your vision will never be more than a dream.

You must know and fully understand this truth: *hope is never enough*. Hope is great, but hope is just one layer of the transformational foundation. If you want to create a complete transformation in any area of your life, you must keep adding layers to the foundation.

Remember, there are *10 Foundational Elements of Transformation*. Each layer will allow you to climb higher and see farther. Each layer must remain in place because it supports the layers above.

Hope simply serves as one layer of the multi-layered foundation that will allow you to add more layers as you move upward and onward. If you keep these layers in place, you will be able to use them to constantly support all areas of your life. Every time you want to be more, do more, have more, accomplish more, or simply make a necessary change in your life for any reason, you must have the necessary foundation in place to support the transformation. Once you understand how each layer is used, you can much more intentionally, effectively, and efficiently use them to support all areas of your life.

This entire book was written to help you navigate your transformational journey. It's a map that will allow you to see what lies ahead. It's a map that reveals the obstacles. It's a map that reveals the most effective and efficient path to transformation.

Like any journey, once you have completed it, you are better equipped to complete it again. You will also be equipped to help others navigate along their path. I have used these foundational elements of transformation many times with great success. I have tested and proven the principles that fill these pages.

At this point in your transformational journey, you must choose to begin leading yourself at a higher level. The most important person you will ever lead is yourself. You must choose to accept full responsibility for making the right choices or the wrong choices as you create your future. Make the right choice, and you get closer to a better future. Make the wrong choice, and you get farther away from what it is you want.

There's a question you need to start asking yourself today. It's a question I will be asking myself regularly for the rest of my life. It's about beginning with the end in mind. It's about taking the right action at the right time for the right reason.

Since I first heard the question, I have never stopped asking it, answering it, acting on it, or sharing it with others. It's the guiding force behind my transformation. This question has allowed me to move from wishing and wondering, to being and doing. It has shaped, and continues to shape, my life.

Every one of us is someplace. However, most of us want to be in a different place. Most of us are uncertain about what to do to move from where we are to where we want to be. The question I'm going to share *assumes you know where you're going*. If you don't know, you need to nail down the answers to the following two sets of questions first. They will help you continue to define and refine your vision.

This first set of questions will establish your *starting point*: "Who am I?" And, "Where am I? The second set of questions will establish your *destination*: "Who do I want to become?" And, "Where do I want to be?"

They also reveal a gap. I call this the "Success Gap." The gap between where you are and where you want to be.

Here's the question you need to learn to ask yourself: *"Will what I'm about to do move me in the right direction?"*

This question is packed full of potential just like you and me! The question is important. The answer is more important. But, your actions are most important.

It's actually a very simple concept. Ask yourself the question when you have a choice to make. If the answer is yes, you do it. If the answer is no, you don't do it. *It says easy, but it does hard*. When the answer is yes, and you follow through, you close the gap. When the answer is no, but you do it anyway, you widen the gap.

"When you decide to pursue greatness, you are taking responsibility for your life. This means that you are choosing to accept the consequences of your actions, and to become the agent of your mental, physical, spiritual, and material success. You may not always be able to control what life puts in your path, but I believe you can always control who you are."
~ Les Brown

12

THE ULTIMATE SACRIFICE

EXTRAORDINARY HEROISM ON DISPLAY

"Courage is fear holding on a minute longer."
~ Gen. George S. Patton

Sergeant First Class Paul Smith gave the ultimate sacrifice. He gave his life in service for others. He took hope to the ultimate level of sacrifice.

On April 4th, 2003 while deployed to Iraq, he was part of a Task Force assigned to build a prisoner of war holding area near the Baghdad International Airport. During this time, he and the Task Force came under attack by a much larger, company size enemy force. Sergeant First Class Smith realized the vulnerability of his Task Force, so he quickly organized a hasty defense consisting of two platoons of soldiers, one Bradley Fighting Vehicle, and three armored personnel carriers.

As the fight developed, Sergeant First Class Smith braved hostile enemy fire to personally engage the enemy with hand grenades and anti-tank weapons. He also organized the evacuation of three wounded soldiers from an armored personnel carrier struck by a rocket propelled grenade and a 60mm mortar round. Seeing the enemy would overrun their defenses, Sergeant First Class Smith moved, under enemy fire, to man a .50 caliber machine gun mounted on a damaged armored personnel carrier. In total disregard for his own life, he maintained his exposed position in order to engage the attacking enemy force.

During this action, he was mortally wounded. His courageous actions helped defeat the enemy attack and resulted in as many as 50 enemy soldiers killed, while allowing the safe withdrawal of numerous wounded soldiers he had been defending.

Sergeant First Class Smith's Congressional Medal of Honor citation speaks of his extraordinary heroism, uncommon valor, and of his hope of making a difference that day. His actions and ultimate sacrifice turned his hope into reality. He made a significant difference in the lives of many others. All sacrifices are not this extreme, but all require some degree of action on our part.

> *"Nothing is more harmful to the service than the neglect of discipline; for it is discipline more than numbers that gives one army superiority over another." ~ George Washington*

SECTION 5

SACRIFICE IS THE FOUNDATION OF DISCIPLINE

13

SACRIFICE IS THE FOUNDATION OF DISCIPLINE

TOO OFTEN, YOU CAN'T REACH WHAT YOU NEED MOST BECAUSE YOU WON'T LET GO OF WHAT YOU WANT MOST

"Everything I've ever let go of has claw marks on it."
~ *David Foster Wallace*

Hope gives you a reason to make sacrifices. But, sacrificing isn't easy. It's hard. It's hard to let go of things and even harder to let go of people. Yes, often to get from where you are to where you want to be, you must sacrifice relationships with people who are not helping you move forward, so you can invest your time with people who will.

Why is sacrifice so hard? Because you feel the loss immediately. And most often, the gain doesn't usually come immediately. The gain may not come for days, weeks, months, or even years. Some among us make sacrifices so others may benefit. These truly special people may *never* see the gain from their sacrifice. They have paid the ultimate price for the ultimate reason: something bigger than themselves. For them, *the sacrifice was the gain.*

Unfortunately, sacrifice alone will not convert your vision into reality. When you sacrifice, you remove things from your life that are preventing you from moving forward. You rid yourself of the things and people that are tapping into your resources such as time, money, and energy. After removing the obstacles, you will be better positioned to make choices that will accelerate your transformation.

Recovering some of your most valuable resources is only half the battle. Once you have made additional resources available, you must intentionally use them to advance toward your preferred future (vision). You must ask and answer the following questions. Then, you must act on the answers.

- How much extra time do I have?
- How can I utilize the extra time?
- How much money have I saved?
- How can I utilize the extra money to create my preferred future?
- How can I be more effective?
- What do I need to start doing?
- What's stopping me from taking action?
- What else do I need to sacrifice?

Let's look at fitness as an example. I often hear many people who want to get fit expressing "legitimate" reasons as to why they can't do it. Here are some of the most common reasons I hear. "I'm too busy." "I don't have the time." "I don't have money to join a gym." All of those may appear to be legitimate, but they are all simply *excuses* given by people who are *unwilling to sacrifice* to get what they want.

When I hear "I'm too busy." or "I don't have the time." I often ask, "Do you watch TV? Do you have any hobbies? Do you spend time with your friends? How long do you sleep? Do you socialize? Do you drink alcohol?" It usually doesn't take long to figure out they are often busy doing something that's not required or that can be sacrificed if they truly want to get fit. These people don't have an issue with time. They have an issue with values. People always make time for the things they value.

When I hear "I don't have the money to join a gym." I often ask, "What does that have to do with getting fit?" These people don't need a gym membership to fit. They need to exercise. Exercise can be done in many places, *if you want to exercise*. It all comes down to one simple principle. People who want to make something happen will find a way. People who don't will find an excuse.

You must make sacrifices to get fit. You must continue to sacrifice to stay fit. And, if you want to go to a higher level of fitness or help others get fit, you will be required to sacrifice even more.

To get from where you are to where you want to be, there are two things you must do. You must develop your character and increase your competency. Those are the only two things that can and will hold you back. What do you want in life? You can have it. However, sacrifices must be made. Are you willing to pay the price? Do you have the discipline to constantly and repeatedly pay the price? Remember, thought is the foundation of choice.

As you discover and move toward your purpose, you will begin to value some things more than others. Then, those things, of lesser value, holding you back will begin to naturally drop away freeing you to intentionally move forward.

"Whenever you see a successful person, you only see the public glories, never the private sacrifices to reach them." ~ Vaibhav Shah

14

SACRIFICE DEMONSTRATES COMMITMENT

WHEN YOU GIVE UP SOMETHING OF LESSER VALUE, YOU ARE POSITIONED TO GAIN SOMETHING OF GREATER VALUE

"The price of anything is the amount of life you exchange for it." ~ Henry David Thoreau

Are you committed to reaching a higher level? Your *words will not* demonstrate your commitment. However, your *sacrifices will*. When you make sacrifices, you are communicating to the world something else is more important. Your actions convey more than a desire for a change. They convey a commitment to change.

As you work to turn your vision for your future into your reality, you will need the help and support of others. The key to gaining the support of others is based in your ability to influence them to help you move forward. When it comes to giving up something, the greater the sacrifice, the greater the influence.

However, people tend to want to keep what they have while trying to get what they want. Most likely, they have already sacrificed something to have what they have. The last thing they want to do is give it up. So, what do they do? They start spending time and energy trying to figure out how they can have both.

Far too often, when people want to get ahead, they

want someone else to make the sacrifice for them. People who aren't willing to pay the price themselves try and get others to pay the price for them. What message does this send to others? Lack of commitment. As a result, influence is diminished.

Many people want their organization to help them or the government to help them. When they can't get the help they think they deserve, they tend to blame those that won't help them. The only person to blame is in the mirror. You are ultimately responsible for your growth. If you won't invest in yourself, why should anyone else?

When you invest in the growth and development of yourself, you are communicating to others a commitment to become more valuable to others. If you choose to invest your money and time on a book, attending a developmental class, or attending a seminar, you will become more valuable, as a result of your sacrifice, to those who value what you're learning. The key is to be sure and inform those you are trying to influence: a current employer/client or a future employer/client.

If you choose to waste your time and money, you also send a message to anyone paying attention. *Your actions always reveal your values.* Wasting your money, time, and energy tells others you're okay with where you are and what you are doing. However, if you're reading this book, I'm going to assume you're not satisfied and want to make a change. If so, it's time to stop talking about changing and start changing.

You must demonstrate your commitment first to yourself, then to others. It's time to make the sacrifice. Stop wasting your time, energy, and money on things and activities that do not increase your value. You *must* begin sacrificing and removing those things from your life.

One of the most dramatic ways to demonstrate

commitment to change is to start by changing who you associate with. That's right. Start by sacrificing personal relationships that are not moving you in the right direction. Why is this so important? Consider Jim Rohn's thoughts in this area, *"We become the combined average of the five people we hang around the most. We start to eat what they eat, drink what they drink, talk like they talk, read what they read, think like they think, watch what they watch, and dress like they dress."* We also tend to get the results they are getting.

Unfortunately for most, relationships are the hardest sacrifice to make. People often stay in bad personal relationships far too long. People also stay in bad professional relationships far too long. Both are detrimental to your preferred future. Change what needs to be changed, not what is easy to change.

Think about it. You most likely have left someone behind in order to be where you are today. They moved on, and you moved on. You changed and developed new relationships. They did too. Life went on. Don't fear change. Fear being stuck in a place you don't want to be.

You will always attract people who are like you. Most important to the attraction is your character. Therefore, if you want to attract people of higher character in your life, you must leave behind those with less character while working to improve your own. The loneliness during the transition is usually the hardest part. Many turn back. But those willing to sacrifice willingly and openly are demonstrating their commitment to a better future.

Make it happen for yourself because no one else can.

"Why do you enter into any activity with anything but commitment to achieve your objective of that activity - not a desire to achieve your objective, but a commitment?" ~ Samuel L. Parker

15

WHEN YOU TOUCH A LIFE, YOU DON'T ALWAYS FEEL IT

WHEN IT COMES TO PEOPLE, THE LITTLE THINGS ARE OFTEN THE BIG THINGS

"A passion for life is contagious and uplifting. Passion cuts both ways... I want to create passion in my own life and with those I care for. I want to feel, experience, and live every emotion. I will suffer through the bad for the heights of the good."
~ Army Ranger, Cpl. Pat Tillman

As a leader of a nonprofit, I (Bren Briggs) hear every day about the brokenness of our heroes and the depression many of them live in every day. But every now and then, I am blessed with stories such as this one that are so moving and positive. I'm happy to share it with you.

Relative to serving our country, many of us in uniform look at what we do as more than a mere job or profession. To many of us, it's a calling. After 28 years of service, I still get choked up every time I hear the National Anthem play, and I get a bit embarrassed when someone says "Thank you for your service."

When Air Force Colonel Rob Maness was called a hero for his valor during the attack on the Pentagon on September 11th, his first reply was that he never considered himself a hero. COL Maness was at the Pentagon when it was attacked. During the mayhem, he was there helping the victims. One of those injured was Army Lieutenant Colonel Birdwell.

LTC Birdwell sustained burns to over 60% of his body, of which, 40% of that was third-degree burns. At some point after being injured and during the initial chaos, he was extricated from the wreckage. He found himself outside the building hooked up to a lifesaving IV being held by none other than COL Maness.

Maness prayed for Birdwell that day and told him he would be ok, but lost track of him afterward.

Due to his extensive injuries, LTC Birdwell spent the next 26 days in intensive care. He had 39 operations over the next four years. 15 years later, and by sheer coincidence, the two met again. However, they weren't immediately aware of their connection to each other.

As each man took a turn telling their story of being at the Pentagon on that tragic day, they quickly realized they were standing next to and talking with the very person they were describing in their own story. I'm sure you can imagine the emotions they both felt at that moment.

Both men have now founded nonprofit organizations. One is on a mission to fight against veteran suicides. The other is on a mission to help burn victims reclaim their lives.

They both understand and have lived, and are still living, a life filled with sacrifice and commitment.

"We need to learn to set our course by the stars, not by the lights of every passing ship." ~ Gen. Omar Bradley

SECTION 6

DISCIPLINE IS THE FOUNDATION OF GROWTH

16

DISCIPLINE IS THE FOUNDATION OF GROWTH

YOU MUST TO DO THE RIGHT THING AT THE RIGHT TIME FOR THE RIGHT REASON

"When it comes to self-discipline, people choose one of two things: Either they choose the pain of discipline, which comes from sacrifice and growth, or they choose the pain of regret, which comes from taking the easy road and missing opportunities."
~ John C. Maxwell

You must develop discipline. Discipline is the catalyst for growth. The more discipline you have, the more growth you will achieve. As you progress from knowing what to do and begin doing what should be done, you are crossing the bridge called discipline. Discipline allows you to turn your dreams, goals, and vision into reality.

Discipline is giving yourself a command and following through with it. You must do the right thing for the right reasons at the right time in order to be effective.

When you take the right steps toward your vision, discipline will allow you to convert your sacrifice into growth. Growth is about reaching and stretching. John C. Maxwell often speaks about the "Law of the Rubber Band" saying, *"People are like rubber bands, we are only adding value when we are being stretched."* Discipline causes you to stretch yourself.

It takes very little effort to stand out in today's society.

Many people in school, college, and the military cannot wait to get finished, get a job, move away from intentional focused learning, and get comfortable.

With discipline, those continuing to educate themselves intentionally by developing their specialized knowledge steadily and consistently increase their potential to do more, earn more, and be more. Consider these impactful words from Napoleon Hill, *"Successful people, in all callings, never stop acquiring specialized knowledge related to their major purpose, business, or profession. Those who are not successful usually make the mistake of believing that the 'knowledge-acquiring' period ends when one finishes school. The truth is that formal education does but little more than to put one in the way of learning how to acquire practical knowledge."*

With discipline, it is not hard to separate yourself from the crowd. Many people don't even attempt to develop and reach their full potential. They simply get comfortable with no desire to grow and stretch themselves any farther. I've read various surveys stating 30-40 percent of high school and college students never read another book after graduation. They lack discipline.

You can easily become exceptional. But, it won't just happen. You must become intentional about developing the discipline that will allow you to make it happen on purpose in pursuit of your vision.

The key is to get into the minds of those already where you want to be. Those already doing what you want to do. You can read books. You may know someone willing to mentor you in person or by phone. As long as you are constantly growing your mind in the area of your passion and purpose, you cannot go wrong.

Humble people understand the more they learn, the more they realize what they have yet to learn. They know they will never learn it all. They see the opportunities for growth ahead. They become disciplined lifetime learners and continue to run the race knowing there truly is no finish line. Having a title, a position, or a degree doesn't mean they have crossed the finish line.

Those who are humble are like sponges soaking up knowledge because they are eager for growth. Who we are determines how we learn, what we learn, and how much we learn. Discipline turns desire into growth.

As you move forward, don't focus on earning more. Focus on *learning* more. Increasing your value is a simple concept. It's always easy to understand, but it's not always easy to do. Discipline is the key.

Your value to others will increase as you read, learn, grow, and apply. It's a never ending process. Do not set a fixed goal and stop after reaching it. You must understand growth is infinite. You want to be growth-oriented, not goal-oriented. Therefore, make *continuous growth* your main goal. Use small, short term goals to support the main goal.

The most important person you will ever influence is yourself. The degree to which you're able to influence yourself will determine the level of influence you ultimately have with others. Typically, when we are talking about leading ourselves, the word most commonly used to describe self-leadership is discipline. You must practice discipline daily to maintain your personal integrity and to increase your influence with others. Discipline is not something you practice only when you feel like it. Discipline is something you practice daily because it's necessary.

> *"The pain of discipline weighs ounces.*
> *Regret ways tons." ~ Jim Rohn*

17

DISCIPLINE LEVERAGES SACRIFICE

THE GREATER THE DISCIPLINE, THE GREATER THE REWARD

"Nothing can stop the man with the right mental attitude from achieving his goals; nothing on earth can help the man with the wrong mental attitude."
~ Thomas Jefferson

The key to moving beyond average is doing what exceptional people do, not wanting what they have. When you see others doing what you want to be doing, the question you must answer is not, "Do I want to be doing what they are doing?" but rather "Do I want to do what they had to do to get to do what they are doing?"

Your answer to the first question communicates you have an interest in doing it. Your answer to the second question communicates if you will have a chance to do it. Deciding to do something and paying the price to actually get to do it is two very different things. Deciding to do something doesn't require sacrifice. However, paying the price to do something will require sacrifice.

Remember, sacrifice is giving up something. The amount of discipline you develop will determine the value you are able to leverage from the sacrifice.

For example, if you decide to enroll in a college class or to attend some type of development seminar, the sacrifice will be the money and the time. Because you are sacrificing your money to grow and develop yourself, you will not be able to use it for anything else. It will be gone. It won't be available for dining out or to put toward a weekend getaway. And, the time you invest in attending the required class(es) cannot be used to do anything else. These are the sacrifices.

The sacrifice only creates an opportunity for growth. It does not create the growth. Only discipline will create growth and allow you to make the additional sacrifices of time necessary to study, learn, and apply what you're learning. Discipline leverages sacrifice. It's a two part formula: SACRIFICE + DISCIPLINE = GROWTH.

The growth cycle must be repeated constantly. Sacrifice something. Demonstrate discipline. Achieve growth. Sacrifice something. Demonstrate discipline. Achieve growth. Sacrifice something. Demonstrate discipline. Achieve growth.

If you have the discipline to repeat the growth cycle, you can become exceptional in your area of interest (passion/purpose) quickly. Why? Because most people will only do what they have to do, which is not much.

Most people can become an expert in their area of passion and purpose in just a few years by simply reading books, magazines, and articles followed by application of what they're learning. Most will not have to attend college or receive any formal education. They must only apply themselves by investing their time instead of wasting their time.

Obviously, if you want to enter a profession that requires a formal education such as practicing law or medicine, you must earn a college degree(s). However, the growth cycle must still be consistently applied. The cycle is a principle for growth. It applies in all situations.

If you don't repeat the growth cycle, you will become stagnant and begin to slip backward. As the world changes at ever increasing speeds, there is no option to remain still. You are either growing or slowing, moving forward or backward. Everything around you is constantly changing. You must also be constantly changing. If not, you may think you're holding steady, but you're not. At some point, you will pay the price for not having the discipline to continue growing and developing yourself as you get passed by those who do.

Another way to leverage sacrifice using discipline is to execute efficiently and effectively. In other words, you must have the discipline to develop an effective plan that allows you to address the most important things you need to learn and do on the front end. You must be methodical and intentional to leverage discipline.

Take the time and do the work necessary to determine what the most important thing that must be done is. Brainstorm a list of all the things you're aware of that must be done to move you from where you are to where you want to be. Then, ask yourself, "What's the most important thing that I must do?" Identify the one thing that if you don't do it, the other things won't matter? Now, do it. If you haven't invested in personal growth and development, that's usually the first place to start.

Too often, people without discipline focus on doing the easy things first. Why? Because it's easy. They jump from one easy thing to the next. Unfortunately, most people who attempt to leverage their sacrifice this way end up wasting their sacrifice. They simply don't have the discipline to do the hard work of doing what's most important first: personal development.

Don't accept your circumstances. Design them.

"We are not victims of our situation.
We are the architects of it." ~ Simon Sinek

18

THE POWER TO PERSEVERE

YOU DON'T ALWAYS GET TO CHOOSE WHAT HAPPENS TO YOU. BUT, YOU ALWAYS GET TO CHOOSE YOUR RESPONSE TO WHAT HAPPENS TO YOU.

"In every battle there comes a time when both sides consider themselves beaten; then he who continues the attack wins." ~ Gen. Ulysses S. Grant

Army Staff Sergeant Matt Lammers knows all about discipline. In 2004, during his first deployment to Iraq, the vehicle he was in hit an Improvised Explosive Device. The IED destroyed the vehicle but not SSGT Lammers. He continued serving his country.

Three years later, while on a routine patrol in Baghdad, the HUMVEE he was traveling in also hit an IED. As a result of the explosion, SSGT Lammers lost both legs and his left arm. At the time of this writing, he is one of only five triple amputees in the nation.

However, Matt Lammers does not focus on what he has lost or what he does not have. And, he loves to swim. Swimming has become his foundation for growth. Like many wounded, ill, and injured Soldiers, Matt found water to be liberating. He often swims without any prosthetics.

Initially and after he learned it was a good method for losing weight, he had the discipline to teach himself to swim. But, in a very short amount of time, Matt started working with a coach and set some new goals to stretch himself.

Today, Matt is a competitive swimmer for Team Army. His coach said, "He is a quintessential example of how sports transcends competition." To date, Matt has a bronze and three gold medals. He has the next Warrior Games squarely in his sites. He even has aspirations of swimming the English Channel.

Matt's motto is: Never give up, never quit. He has made many sacrifices. However, it's his laser focused discipline that has allowed him to leverage those sacrifices. As a result, he has grown himself into a world class, and very competitive, Paralympic swimmer.

> *"I will never quit. My nation expects me to be physically harder and mentally stronger than my enemies. If knocked down I will get back up, every time. I will draw on every remaining ounce of strength. I am never out of the fight."*
> *~ Navy Seal, Marcus Luttrell*

SECTION 7

GROWTH IS THE FOUNDATION OF CHANGE

19

GROWTH IS THE FOUNDATION OF CHANGE

IF YOU'RE NOT GROWING, YOU'RE SLOWING

"When I go through change it is because I am passive; I accept it as an inevitable. So, I sigh and say, I hope this comes out all right. When I grow through change, I become active. I take control of my attitude, my emotions. Years ago, I determined that while others may lead small lives, I would not; while others may become victims, I would not; and while others will leave their future in other's hands, I will not. And while others go through life, I will grow through it. That is my choice, and I will surrender it to no one."
~ John C. Maxwell

You can change without growing. However, you can't grow without changing. You can create change or be impacted by change caused by others. Change may, and often does, just happen. Most change is outside of your control.

Growth is much different. Growth doesn't just happen. It doesn't simply come with age. If it did, all of the older people would be more successful than all of the younger people. That's simply not how it works. You must make a choice to be intentional about your growth.

As you continue learning about *The 10 Foundational Elements of Transformation*, understand all the foundational layers you've learned so far support your growth. The foundational layer of growth that's just been added will support the following foundational layers: change, success, significance, and legacy. Each layer is supported by those that come before it. And, each layer helps support all of those that come after it.

This book was written in a methodical and sequential way to support you in any area where you desire change and transformation. It's sequentially assembled to allow you to better understand how the various layers support and are supported by each other. The principles you're learning can be applied to any area of your life, personally and professionally.

Let's refer back to the previous example of fitness. You will not become fit accidentally. No one else can make you fit. You must do it. Likewise, you will not grow accidentally. No one else can grow you. You will always be responsible for growing yourself. These thoughts bring to mind a quote from an unknown source, *"You can lead a human to knowledge, but you can't make them think."*

You must develop an intentional growth plan that will move you toward your vision. As you move along the path of transformation, you will be able see more and see farther. As you expand your vison, you must also make adjustments to your growth plan to remain highly effective and efficient. Intentional growth based on your passion will always lead you closer to discovering your *why*, your purpose.

Remember, you will be much more effective if you are primarily growth-oriented and secondarily goal-oriented. That does not mean you do not set goals. You should always set goals that support your *continuous* growth. Keep in mind, the goal of growth is not change for the sake of change. Change can be positive or negative. Negative change will not serve you well.

The goal of growth is positive change. What determines if change is positive? Positive change moves you closer to realizing your vision, creating your preferred future, and allows you to live a life more closely aligned with your purpose.

Where will you see the most benefit when your growth leads to change? Character growth will always produce the greatest results because it acts as a multiplier relative to your competency. Relative to character, you will see the most positive change when you work in areas of *weakness*. When it comes to growing and developing your character, focus on developing your integrity, not creating your image.

The second area where your growth will show up is in your competency. However, when working to create positive change relative to your competency, you should always work in areas of *strength* where you are naturally gifted. Character will take you most of the way, and competency will take you the rest of the way.

It's worth mentioning again. As you grow, you will likely need to leave some people behind. They may not be going where you're going. You may be able to influence them to grow with you. If not, you should not allow them to hold you back. They make their choices. You make your choices. You can still love them while you're missing them. Your journey through life is not their journey through life. We're all on a different mission.

To live more abundantly, you must move forward.

"Where there is no belief or hope for growth to be real, it is no longer attempted. People, or organizations, enter into a state of sameness, and as we have seen, that is really when things are no longer alive. Death is taking over not growth." ~ Dr. Henry Cloud

20

GROWTH CREATES OPTIONS

WHEN YOU GROW YOURSELF, YOU ATTRACT NEW OPPORTUNITIES

"The moment you take responsibility for everything in your life is the moment you can change anything in your life." ~ Hal Elrod

Growth will *always* increase your influence. When you increase your influence, you *will* increase your options.

Instead of taking the risk of investing in themselves along the way, too many people play it safe and invest in their retirement. They value having money and comfort later instead of growth and options now. The result: many people live an unfilled, safe, *and often miserable*, life dreaming about the opportunity to escape from it all, to retire, to truly quit living and start waiting. *Waiting to die.*

That is not a life. That is an existence. What's stopping you from living a better and more fulfilling life today?

Most people seek *security* and *stability* in their lives. However, what they need in order to truly excel, become the best version of themselves, and create their preferred future is *freedom* and *options*.

You must continuously follow your passion to find your purpose. If you don't like what you're doing, why are you doing it? There's only one reason, you don't have options? Why? You're not focused on growing. You're focused on coasting. I read the following on a sign outside a church many years ago, *"If the truth hurts, it probably should."*

Too many of us think we're on a journey, but we're not. We may have started out strong, but as we went farther down the path and things got harder, we took a seat on the first bench we saw and have been there ever since watching others pass us by. If you're on the bench, it's time for you to get up, get going again, and make a bigger difference in the world.

Don't know where to start? Start with your world, the one best seen when looking in a mirror. Start with you.

Most of your options will not be created between 9am and 5pm. While you're busy working, someone else is in control. Someone else is determining your agenda. They are paying you to do what they want done. There's not a lot of time for intentional growth and development.

If you're serious about creating options for yourself, you must create them between 5pm and 9am. You decide what you do when you're not at work. What you do when you're not at work determines when you work, how much you work, what work you do, and how much you get paid to work. This is where sacrifice and discipline are key to your growth. How you spend or invest your time away from work is up to you. What needs to change?

When it comes to increasing your options, you can work in the area of character or competency. Several research studies have revealed **87% of our results/influence come from our character** and only 13% of our results/influence come from our competency.

Before you get to do what it is you want to do, you must influence someone to give you a chance. The key to getting the chance will first be based on your character. However, it often takes time to learn someone's true character. Therefore, some people with character issues are given a chance they don't deserve. In this case, it is later taken away. People are usually hired for what they know (competency), but often they are later fired for who they are (character).

As you become intentional about growth, you should invest 80% of your time and resources on character development. Your character growth will allow you to attract others with higher level character. Others who can help you. Others who have greater influence than those with less character. The more you develop your character, the better your social network will become.

Intentionally invest the other 20% of your time and resources on competency development. Focus on the areas you're naturally interested in and gifted in. No one can compete with someone who has a passion and a fire burning inside them. Don't flow with the current. Choose your destination.

You may not be doing what you want to do now. That's okay. Start where you are and grow your way to where you want to be. As you work on your character and develop your competency in your area of interest, you will naturally start to attract others with the same interest. As you do, you will be presented with new opportunities and options. The opportunities are there waiting for you.

Then, if you're willing to continue sacrificing and growing, you will begin to reshape your career and be well on your way to creating your preferred future.

"On the path to your God-inspired future, attractive alternatives will be offered. You will be presented with more money, a better position, or a more sedate lifestyle in a more comfortable geographic location. You are going to face other kinds of more dramatic temptations as well. We all do. But, we have to constantly remember our future." ~ Terry A. Smith

21

STAYING POSITIVE THROUGH IT ALL

PERSONAL GROWTH HAPPENS WHEN YOU CHOOSE POSITIVE RESPONSES IN NEGATIVE SITUATIONS

"Now more than ever, we must stop preparing for past battles and prepare for new ones."
~ *Capt. D. Michael Abrashoff*

The supporting stories at the end of each section have been added to help encourage, engage, and empower you to lead yourself and your life at a higher level. Our intended purpose is to help you see that many things are possible, once YOU choose to make it happen. Remember: Thoughts + Emotions + Action = Choice.

Staff Sergeant Brian Baker provides us with a great example. He has applied this formula in his life, and it worked. SSGT Baker had several deployments in his career. During his 2008 deployment to Afghanistan, he experienced situation after situation where a normal person might have easily broken and started making bad choices. However, he intentionally chose to grow in a positive direction through it all.

It all started during a routine patrol. His unit was hit by an IED. In the immediate aftermath, he was ran over and dragged some distance by an Afghanistan National Police vehicle which resulted in torn ligaments and muscles in his right shoulder, several broken ribs, and a

TBI (Traumatic Brain Injury). That wasn't enough to stop him. It was still mission first for SSGT Baker.

He continued to push on despite his injuries and against medical advice. Days later, SSGT Baker began experiencing chest pains. Again, he was directed to a medevac. Since there were no replacements, he continued to put the mission and his Soldiers first. SSGT Baker chose once again to remain and carry out the mission.

After several more missions, SSGT Baker was once again hit by an IED. Unfortunately, things were different this time. This incident required him to be medically evacuated. As a result of his injuries, SSGT Baker spent the next few years at a WTB (Warrior Transition Battalion) in Fort Bragg North Carolina.

As with many wounded warriors in this same situation, SSGT Baker's wife decided divorce was the best option for her. She proceeded to file for divorce while he was still recovering from his injuries. SSGT Baker could have grown bitter. He could have grown cold and hostile, but he chose a different path.

SSGT Baker is far better now because of the conscious, intentional, and positive choices he made throughout all of the adversity he faced. Today, he is a successful contractor. He still has his moments, as we all do, but his character and intentional focus on personal growth has given him an advantage and prepared him for all of life's challenges.

"The supreme quality for leadership is unquestionably integrity. Without it, no real success is possible, no matter whether it is on a section gang, a football field, in an army, or in an office."
~ Gen. Dwight D. Eisenhower

SECTION 8

GROWTH IS THE FOUNDATION OF SUCCESS

22

CHANGE IS THE FOUNDATION OF SUCCESS

IF YOU ALREADY KNEW WHAT YOU NEED TO KNOW, YOU WOULD ALREADY BE WHERE YOU WANT TO GO

"Those who cannot change their minds cannot change anything." ~ George Bernard Shaw

Without change, there can be no improvement. But, as you've already learned, the change you seek should be positive. Negative change will not bring about success. The change being discussed on these pages is the change created by your intentional growth. Positive change created by you.

Changing doesn't mean you will become successful. You must change the right things for the right reasons. If you truly want success, don't focus on changing to become successful. Focus first on changing to become more valuable. As you become more valuable, you *will* become more successful. The most valuable people are also the most successful people.

Creating positive change takes courage. I remember the words of Anais Nin, *"Life shrinks or expands in proportion to one's courage."* Positive change begins as thoughts in the mind. But, it's courage that will allow you to convert those thoughts into positive change.

The remainder of this chapter is an excerpt from my

book, *Change Happens: Leading Yourself and Others Through Change*, which I co-authored with my wife, Ria Story.

Change has the power to launch you into a new career, a new relationship, a new city, and even a new way of thinking. When you change what you do, you change what you get. Saying *no* to the *wrong* things frees you up to say *yes* to the *right* things. What you say yes to *shapes* your future. Saying no to something old gives you the *freedom* to say yes to something new.

Without the courage to change, you will get left behind by those brave enough to take risks and fail their way to a better future. Failure isn't really the appropriate word to use. Failure is actually often misused. People use the word failure as an excuse not to try something. However, it's only failure if you quit and never try again.

As a baby, you fell endless times as you attempted to walk. Try. Fail. Try. Fail. Try. Fail. But, that's not really what happened. In the end, did you fail to walk, or did you learn to walk? You learned to walk like the rest of us.

What really happened was this. Try. Learn. Try. Learn. Try. Learn. Try. Succeed. Find something new to learn. Repeat.

The rest of life should be the same way. It took courage then, and it'll take even more courage to try new things now. Why? Because when you were learning to walk, you received endless encouragement from everyone around you. And most often, when you would fall, someone would pick you up. Learning as an adult is a bit harder.

Things are different once you grow up. As an adult, you will mostly receive a lot of doubting questions and negative feedback from other adults. If babies could talk and understand each other, they would probably never learn to walk. Could you imagine what it would be like in the nursery listening to the babies talking?

- Why do you want to walk?
- Don't you think you might fall?
- I tried that once, and it didn't work.
- Have you considered what will happen if you do fall? I bet it will really hurt!
- I saw Danny try that last week. He fell, broke his nose, and cried for hours.
- Have you thought about what will happen once you get going? How will you stop?

I was having a little fun with you, but I'm sure you get the point. That's what adults do all day long. You've heard those voices. They try to talk other adults out of trying something new because they're afraid themselves. If you want to get to a new level, you've got to change how you invest your time and who you invest it with.

You need to be reading, watching videos, or listening to audios of people who are doing what you want to be doing or that have done what you want to do. Whatever you do, don't seek advice about your life and your future from anyone who has not been where you want to go.

They don't know how to get there, and they don't want to go. Why would you ever give them a right to veto your dream? You shouldn't. Don't do it!

"The first step toward success is taken when you refuse to be a captive of the environment you first find yourself in." ~ Mark Caine

23

CHANGE RELEASES POTENTIAL

WITHOUT CHANGE, YOUR POTENTIAL CAN NEVER BECOME YOUR REALITY

"When we are faced with change, we either step forward into growth, or we step backward into safety." ~ Abraham Maslow

Are you playing small? What are you leaving on the table? Your potential is your reality. You can verify this because where you are now is not where you used to be? Why? You have already realized some of your potential, your untapped reality. Therefore, your potential today can also become your reality tomorrow.

Georg Lichtenburg made the following observation, *"I cannot say whether things will get better if we change; what I can say is they must change if they are to get better."* When everything is constantly changing, the challenge is also changing. What was mastered successfully yesterday may no longer be relevant today. Therefore, the one thing that should also constantly change is *you* and *me*. If we're not willing to change, we should expect to be left behind by those that are.

When we choose to constantly change to meet new challenges, we have a chance to continue to achieve personal and organizational success. But, when we refuse to change in response to new and greater challenges, we and the organizations where we work will struggle to survive, and some will end up taking a dive.

Just as you were able to leverage sacrifice for your benefit, you can also leverage change for your benefit. Leverage (the verb) is defined as "using a quality or advantage to obtain a desired result."

As Ria Story wrote in *Change Happens*, *"When we leverage something, we take advantage of the lever to multiply the results of our efforts. Leveraging something can be a powerful way to gain momentum and accelerate progress. But, we seldom think of change as something we can, or should, leverage."* If you're not leveraging change, you're missing a great opportunity to accelerate your journey to a higher level of success.

Ria continues, *"Change always brings opportunities. When we leverage change we not only take advantage of the obvious opportunities, we create new ones as well. In order to leverage change and take advantage of or create opportunities, we first must see them. Then, we must be willing to put forth the effort to maximize them."*

When it comes to change, who will potentially receive the most benefit? Someone who resists change or someone who embraces change? No doubt, the person embracing change will be more likely to turn their potential into success. Once you've made the choice to embrace change, don't stop there.

As you begin leveraging change, there will be many benefits that will help you achieve greater success. Leverage the change for maximum benefit. Leveraging change means doing more than simply making the change. Leveraging change means you will seek ways to intentionally grow your influence during the change.

Those who are neutral or resistant to change will never receive the benefits associated with leveraging change. As you already know, most people don't like change and put their energy into resisting and complaining. When others are moaning, groaning, and whining, it's easy for you to start shining.

As Denis Waitley remarked, *"A sign of wisdom and maturity is when you come to terms with the realization that your decisions cause your rewards and consequences. You are responsible for your life, and your ultimate success depends on the choices you make."* When you choose to be proactive while everyone else is being reactive, that mindset is already allowing you to leverage change to your benefit. By changing the way you think, you're able to turn your potential into success.

High impact leaders intentionally embrace, leverage, and initiate change. They are also aware of others who do the same. You can unleash your potential when you focus on increasing your influence with game changers. They operate at an entirely different level and tend to operate with others who exhibit the same level of character when it comes to change.

When it comes to leveraging change there's a magic word you can proactively use to begin separating yourself from the crowd in a way that allows you to get *noticed* by the high impact leaders and *promoted* for the right reasons. The magic word is "HOW."

When you ask, "How can I?" or "How can we?" instead of "Can I?" or "Can we?" you have started to truly transform the way you and others think. "Can I?" indicates self-doubt. You don't know if you can. But, when you say "How can I?" you have already decided you will and you can. Therefore, your imagination can run wild in the right direction. "How can I?" lets you know there is a way. You just need to discover it.

"Small, Smart Choices + Consistency + Time = RADICAL DIFFERENCE" ~ Darren Hardy

24

ONE MORE DAY

UNTIL YOU GIVE UP, YOU HAVE NOT FAILED.

"Retreat? Hell, we just got here!"
~ Capt. Lloyd Williams"

In the summer of 1966, a small unit of Marines and two Navy Corpsmen were left on Hill 488. Their mission was to watch for enemy troop movement and to call in artillery and air strikes as needed. After about three days, the unit's commander began to sense it was time to remove the small unit. However, the Staff Sergeant in charge, SSGT Howard, requested one more day.

As it turned out, the enemy forces had discovered their position and were moving a very large (200-250 man unit) and well trained force toward their position. Unfortunately, it was too late in the evening to evacuate the 16 Marines and two Navy Corpsmen.

At 10 o'clock that night, the sky lit up with enemy fire from small arms, grenades, mortars, and support from four .50 caliber machine guns. The Marines pulled back into a smaller defensive position about 20 yards in diameter. Back-to-back, they began to defend their small perimeter as they counted on each other to work as a team to do the impossible. They were outnumbered by more than 10 to 1, but the leadership and inspiration of SSGT Howard was all that was needed to sustain them.

Several of the Marines were injured, and a few were killed in the initial assault. They all knew there would be additional assaults as long as they continued to occupy Hill 488. SSGT Howard called his commander for an evacuation, but there would be none that night. They were on their own. In order to survive, he would have to continue to lead his men until the following day when it would be possible for a helicopter to reach them.

All night long, they fought fiercely repelling assault after assault not losing even an inch of ground. As SSGT Howard conducted an ammunition check, he discovered they were out of grenades. He also discovered the other ammunition was critically low. What did he do? He issued one of the most unusual orders in combat history, "Throw rocks!"

As unbelievable as the order sounded, it worked. When the enemy soldiers began to push their way through the sparse brush, the Marines began to throw rocks at them as ordered. Mistaking the rocks for grenades, the enemy soldiers moved into the open providing clear and accurate shots. As a result, the Marines made the most of the remaining rounds of ammunition.

During one of the assaults, SSGT Howard was shot in the back and couldn't move his legs. As the enemy continued to assault his perimeter, the wounded leader did his best to also continue to encourage his Marines. He kept reminding them if they could hold out until daylight more Marines would come in and extract them.

The next day came, and Hill 488 was still taking enemy fire. A rescue attempt failed when the chopper was shot down, but a Marine company was also on the way to rescue SSGT Howard and his men.

Around noon the next day, the company finally

reached SSGT Howard and his men. Five of his men had been killed, but amazingly, 12 of them had survived. When it was all over, they had eight rounds of ammunition between them.

"When you are commanding, leading soldiers under conditions where physical exhaustion and privations must be ignored, where the lives of soldiers may be sacrificed, then, the efficiency of your leadership will depend only to a minor degree on your tactical ability. It will primarily be determined by your character, your reputation, not much for courage—which will be accepted as a matter of course—but by the previous reputation you have established for fairness, for that high-minded patriotic purpose, that quality of unswerving determination to carry through any military task assigned to you."
~ Gen. George C. Marshall"

SECTION 9

SUCCESS IS THE FOUNDATION OF SIGNIFICANCE

25

SUCCESS IS THE FOUNDATION OF SIGNIFICANCE

TO BE SUCCESSFUL, YOU MUST FOCUS ON BECOMING MORE VALUABLE, NOT MORE SUCCESSFUL

"Your ability to achieve your own happiness is the true measure of your success in life. Nothing is more important. Nothing can replace it. If you accomplish everything of a material nature, but you are not happy, you have actually "failed" at fulfilling your potential as a human being." ~ Brian Tracy

The most successful people are those who help others become successful. However, until you create a high level of success for yourself, it's not likely that you will be in a position to help others become highly successful. The remainder of this book is intended to help you understand what it truly means to be successful, significant, and ultimately, to leave a legacy.

If you choose to develop the habits of success, you'll make success a habit. Successful people have the habit of intentionally investing time and money into growing themselves because they value themselves and know this truth: Life IS hard! So, they take responsibility to make life a little easier by developing themselves. As a result, they are able to *acheive better results*.

When it comes to creating success, the words of Norman Vincent Peale ring true, *"Believe in yourself! Have faith in your abilities! Without a humble but reasonable confidence in your powers, you cannot be successful or happy."* This is why the habit of intentionally growing and developing yourself is key. Your growth in your area of passion and purpose will give you confidence. You will quickly separate yourself from those who are coasting through life.

No matter how much someone else believes in you, you must ultimately believe in yourself. You can borrow belief from others to get going, but to be highly effective, you must believe in yourself. You can generate this belief and confidence from within by simply leading yourself well in the direction you want to go.

The byproduct of growth and development is belief and confidence. The byproduct of belief and confidence is success. Consider the wisdom in the words of St. Francis of Assisi, *"Start doing what is necessary; then, do what is possible; and suddenly you are doing the impossible."* To be successful, you must start where you are and do what you can. Do this consistently and endlessly, and you will become highly successful. Discipline is the key to success.

Do you dream about a higher level of success?

This question reminds me of a story about an old Army general sitting at the bar of an officer's club staring at his third martini. A brand-new second lieutenant comes in and spots him. He can't resist sitting next to the general and starting up a conversation. The old general patiently listens to the kid and courteously answers his questions. After a time, the second lieutenant gets to what he really wants to know. "How do you make general?" he asks with raw, unconcealed ambition.

"Well son," said the old general, "here's what you do. You work like a dog, you never stop studying, you train your troops hard, and you take care of them. You are loyal to your commander and your soldiers. You do the best you can in every mission, and you love the Army. You are ready to die for the mission and your troops. That's all you have to do."

The second lieutenant replied with a soft, young voice, "Wow, and that's how you make general?"

"Naw!" bellowed the old general. "That's how you make first lieutenant. Just keep doing all of the things I told you and let 'em see what you've got," said the general, finishing off his last martini as he turned to walk away.

The old general was saying to the young second lieutenant that in order to be successful he would need to make a career out of serving others. The general told him to start with development of himself. Then, grow and develop others. Then, serve everyone. Oh, and be willing to sacrifice for the mission and your team if necessary. That's what serving looks like through the eyes of an old general. He basically gave a class about success and significance in just a few short sentences.

Success looks different for everyone. Don't measure yourself against others who appear successful. For you to be successful, you simply must be better tomorrow than you are today as you strive to turn your vision for a preferred future into reality. That is success. When you're able to move from where you are and get closer to where you want to be, you're traveling down the road to success.

Success will always create momentum, and momentum will always create the opportunity for more success.

"When a challenge in life is met by a response that is equal to it, you have success. But when the challenge moves to a higher level, the old, once successful response no longer works - it fails; thus, nothing fails like success." ~ Dr. Stephen R. Covey

26

SUCCESS CREATES MOMENTUM

WHEN YOU CREATE MOMENTUM, DON'T REST ON IT. BUILD UPON IT.

"Where success is concerned, people are not measured in inches, or pounds, or college degrees, or family background; they are measured by the size of their thinking. How big we think determines the size of our accomplishments." ~ David Schwartz

When it comes to achieving success, momentum is your best friend. As with sacrifice and change, momentum can also be leveraged. When you're able to generate momentum, don't miss the opportunity to leverage it for additional success. Your goal should always be to *maximize momentum*.

Far too often, when someone creates momentum, the first thing they tend to do is take it easy and coast for a while. Don't allow yourself to fall into that trap. Creating momentum when there is none is much more difficult than sustaining momentum when there is some. When you've done the hard work of creating it, leverage it.

When you are successful, you will have more energy, more confidence, more people paying attention, and more opportunities. Let's look at how you can leverage momentum in each of these areas.

When you have more energy, you will feel better. When you feel better you're more likely to be motivated to make additional things happen. Instead of celebrating how great you feel, by taking some time away from your mission, channel the energy into the next project or a new opportunity for growth. Use the energy you've gained to do something you've been putting off because you didn't feel like it. Just do it. This will leverage the energy created by momentum.

When you achieve success, you will have more confidence. Success breeds success. With a greater level of confidence, you will see things differently. Step back and consider your options for continuing to move yourself forward. Things that were not previously on your radar will suddenly appear. Use the confidence you have to stretch yourself in areas where you lacked confidence before. Move beyond your comfort zone and try something completely new. This will leverage the confidence created by momentum.

When you're making things happen, people are likely to notice. People will see you moving forward. They will be more likely to want to help you or be helped by you. Most often, both will happen. Gaining support will give you a boost. Helping others will give you a boost. When others want to help you more or be helped more because of your success, you're leveraging the visibility created by momentum.

When you're successful, people will talk about you. They will praise you. They will recommend you. Ultimately, others who believe what you believe and are interested in what you're interested in will notice you. As a result, you will have more opportunities which can lead to additional success. When you act on new opportunities because of past results, you are leveraging the opportunity created by momentum.

There's something you want to do, something you want to accomplish. Don't wait because as Karen Lamb said, *"A year from now, you will wish you had started today."*

The most successful people intentionally create momentum and never lose it. Once they get started, they never stop. They know creating momentum is like trying to roll a large heavy object such as an automobile. It takes a tremendous amount of energy to get it going, but it takes much less energy to keep it going. Your climb to the next level will be very much the same.

You may struggle at first to figure out who you want to become and where you want to be. This is often the hardest part of intentional growth, but it's necessary. Zig Ziglar said it best, *"Growth is painful. Change is painful. But, nothing is as painful as being stuck somewhere you don't belong."* However, once you're able to clearly define your vision, pay the price, and actually start moving in the right direction, you're able to continue down the path with much less effort.

Your success will not only benefit you. As you create momentum, your success will begin to positively impact the lives of those around you at home and at work. The ultimate way to leverage momentum in your own life is to help others create momentum in their lives. When you begin to intentionally impact the lives of others positively, you are maximizing momentum. It is no longer about your journey. It is about you helping others along their journey.

Achieving your own personal success must come first because you must steady yourself before you can support and lift others. There's no greater success than helping someone else become successful.

"Before you are a leader, success is all about growing yourself. When you become a leader, success is all about growing others." ~ Jack Welch

27

SHOWDOWN IN THE SKY

YOU CAN NEVER WIN BY GIVING UP

"There can be no retreat when there's no rear. You can't retreat, or even withdraw, when you're surrounded. The only thing you can do is to break out, and in order to do that you have to attack, and that is what we're about to do." ~ Maj. Gen. Oliver P. Smith

On June 30, 1953, Air Force Colonel Johnson was leading a flight of four fighter aircraft deep within enemy territory when a flight of 12 enemy aircraft appeared. Colonel Johnson immediately initiated an attack and focused on destroying one of the enemy aircraft.

Closing on the single enemy aircraft, Colonel Johnson held his fire until he was within twelve hundred feet, at which time he landed numerous hits on the enemy aircraft. To assure he did not lose his tactical advantage and with full knowledge of the potential danger from the other MIGS in the enemy flight, Colonel Johnson continued his attack.

With unswerving singleness of purpose, Colonel Johnson began firing from a range of six hundred feet. He continued his devastating barrage until he was only fifty feet from the enemy aircraft, at which time it began to burn and disintegrate. Only then did Colonel Johnson turn to face the attack of the other enemy aircraft.

While expertly maneuvering to escape the attacking enemy, Colonel Johnson experienced a loss of engine power. In spite of the damage to his aircraft, he valiantly turned to attack the enemy while maintaining his momentum.

With superb airmanship and aggressiveness, he outmaneuvered them until they withdrew from the area. Momentum allows us to perform at a higher level.

> *"It doesn't take a hero to order men into battle. It takes a hero to be one of those men who goes into battle." ~ Gen. H. Norman Schwarzkopf*

SECTION 10

SIGNIFICANCE IS THE FOUNDATION OF LEGACY

28

SIGNIFICANCE IS THE FOUNDATION OF LEGACY

SUCCESS IS ABOUT GETTING RESULTS, SIGNIFICANCE IS ABOUT HELPING OTHERS GET RESULTS

"We build and defend not for our generation alone. We defend the foundations laid by our fathers. We build a life for generations yet unborn. We defend and we build a way of life, not for America alone, but for all mankind." ~ Franklin D. Roosevelt

Success is all about you, what you have achieved, and what you will achieve. However, to make a greater impact, you must shift your focus to significance which is all about helping others become successful. Significance is not about how far you advance yourself, significance is about how far you advance others.

The most successful people do not settle for success. They hunger for more. Not for themselves, but for others. They understand success is just a stepping stone along the path toward significance. As John C. Maxwell observed, *"Once you have tasted significance, nothing else will satisfy you."*

With significance, what started out as a simple vision for your own personal growth has now compounded into a vision to help others achieve and succeed. You no longer have to only sacrifice for yourself. Your vision is now much bigger than you. Therefore, if you want to truly experience significance, you must begin sacrificing for the benefit of others with hopes they too will someday choose a life of significance.

However, most aren't willing to sacrifice for themselves, much less others. The few who are willing to sacrifice for others will move far beyond success and live a life of significance. Those who have achieved significance will not leave a legacy for others. They will leave a legacy *in* others.

5 Signs You Have Reached Significance
(Adapted from my book, *10 Values of High Impact Leaders*)

1. **You can never learn enough.** You're not focused on a formal education. There is no graduation date. You're focused on a lifetime of learning and growing. You're not concerned with the generalized knowledge the masses possess. You know your passion and have found your purpose. As a result, you are laser focused on developing highly specialized knowledge in your area of giftedness.
2. **You help others climb the ladder.** Your concern has moved beyond your own success. You're now focused on the success of others. Because you're a lifetime learner with specialized knowledge, you are uniquely positioned to help others, who value what you value, climb more efficiently and effectively up the ladder of success. You are rare! Instead of selfishly hoarding knowledge, you share it intentionally with others.
3. **You help others become wealthy.** Not only do you help others climb the ladder of success, but you also help them become more valuable. You teach them

this secret: "If you want to be a success, don't focus on becoming successful. Focus on becoming more valuable." You know true wealth does not mean having money. True wealth is having the ability to produce wealth.

4. **You seek growth.** You know real growth is a result of personal growth. You apply the 80/20 rule in this area. You spend 80% of your time working on areas of weakness relative to your character. You spend the other 20% of your time working on areas of strength relative to your competency. You know research studies have shown 87% of your results come from character and 13% come from competency. You know all of your growth happens outside your comfort zone.

5. **You never want to retire.** Because of your endless personal growth and highly developed specialized knowledge, you no longer have a career. You've found your calling, what you were put on this earth to do. You are in the zone and can no longer distinguish between work and play. It's all the same. You love what you do, and you look forward to doing it. Not just for now, but forever. The thought of retiring doesn't even cross your mind. Instead of wondering when you can retire, you wonder how long you can keep going.

When you choose a life of significance, you've chosen to live life at a higher level. Who you are matters.

"I dare you, whoever you are, share with others the fruits of your daring. Catch a passion for helping others and a richer life will come back to you".
~ William H. Danforth

29

SIGNIFICANCE IS NOT ABOUT YOU, BUT IT STARTS WITH YOU.

WHO YOU ARE ON THE INSIDE IS WHAT OTHERS EXPERIENCE ON THE OUTSIDE

"Talent is God-given. Be humble.
Fame is man-given. Be grateful.
Conceit is self-given. Be careful."
~ John Wooden

When you choose a life of significance, your life is no longer just about you and what you have accomplished. Significance is far bigger than any one individual. Significance is about touching the lives of others in a way that what you leave in them flows into others. When you achieve significance your influence is magnified by others and multiplied through others. Significance will never be about you, but significance will always start with you.

As you reflect back on what you've learned, you should now be able to see the big picture, a picture that may not have been visible as you started reading this book. However, you should be able to see the roadmap of transformation more clearly now. *I highly recommend reading this book again with the big picture in mind.*

The roadmap of transformation begins with values and ends with legacy. How far you travel down the road of transformation is up to you. Your choices will determine the distance you're able to travel and the speed you're able to travel. Ultimately, who you are will determine how far and how fast you go.

What you choose to value on the inside will reveal your character to those on the outside. In the words of Andy Stanley, *"There is no cramming for a test of character. It is always a pop quiz. You're either ready or you're not. It's the law of the harvest at work. In the moment of testing, you will reap what you have sown."* I define character as: thinking, feeling, and acting in a congruent way while making excellent moral and ethical choices based on self-evident natural laws and principles.

Mahadev Desai, Mahatma Gandhi's secretary, when asked how Gandhi could speak for hours, without notes, while mesmerizing his audiences said, *"What Gandhi thinks, what he feels, what he says, and what he does are all the same. He does not need notes. You and I, we think one thing, feel another, say a third, and do a fourth, so we need notes and files to keep track."*

Desai was describing what it means to be congruent. Gandhi walked the talk. His actions matched his words in everything he did. He was real. He was a whole person.

In all that you do, you need to not only be congruent with what comes out of your mouth, but also what comes out of your heart. You must work constantly to align your words, actions, beliefs, and values with natural laws and principles. Your ability to live in harmony with these natural laws and principles will determine the level of trust you are able to build with others along your transformational journey.

Trust is the key to influence. Influence is the key to relationships. And ultimately, relationships are the key to your success and your ability to live a life of significance. In order to build trust on the outside, you must develop your character on the inside. Whenever I think of character, I'm reminded of the words of John Luther, *"Good character is more to be praised than outstanding talent. Most talents are, to some extent, a gift. Good character, by contrast, is not given to us. We have to build it piece by piece: by thought, choice, courage, and determination."*

Every chapter in this book is filled with principles to help you build your character. Regardless, of where we are in our lives, we all have the ability to improve our character. Your character will either accelerate you or anchor you. It will propel you along your journey or weigh you down as you try to reach and stretch your way to the next level of success on your way to significance.

Many people don't understand the word character. Dr. Henry Cloud's definition of character and integrity is simple enough, *"Character is the ability to meet the demands of reality. Integrity is the courage to meet the demands of reality."* When you can't achieve what you want to achieve, the cause can always be traced back to a character flaw.

Character doesn't simply mean good or bad. The absolute best person you know has character flaws. Having character flaws does not make you bad. Having character flaws makes you human. Character is key.

Your legacy will be defined by your character. It will be defined by what you leave behind within others. What will determine if your vision becomes your legacy? It won't be you. It will be those who felt valued by you. It will be those who were able to allow your influence to pass through them into the lives of others.

"When you do the common things in life in an uncommon way, you will command the attention of the world." ~ George Washington Carver

30

25 MINUTES THAT CHANGED HISTORY

YOUR CHARACTER IS NOT DEVELOPED UNDER FIRE, IT IS REVEALED

"There's no quitting, I can't have quit in me. There was never an option to stop and quit." ~ Maj. Lisa Jaster

History was made when a 23 year old female Kentucky National Guardsmen received a medal, the Silver Star. Sergeant Leigh Ann Hester of the 617th Military Police Company received the Silver Star along with two other members of her unit, Staff Sergeant Timothy Nein and Specialist Jason Mike.

Their day started as any other day, with a routine patrol and route clearing mission. However, that day would end like no other day had. The squad SGT Hester was assigned to was shadowing a supply convoy on March 20, 2005 when approximately 50 enemy fighters ambushed the convoy near Salman Pak. The squad moved to the side of the road, flanking the insurgents to cut off their escape route.

SGT Hester led her team through the kill zone and into a flanking position where she assaulted a trench line with grenades and a M203 grenade-launcher. She and SSGT Nein, her squad leader, then proceeded to clear two trenches. SGT Hester killed three insurgents at that time. When the fight was over, 27 insurgents were dead, six were wounded, and one was captured.

Three soldiers of the 617th were wounded in the ambush. SGT Hester said she and the other squad members think about them every day. She also said the firefight, along with the entire deployment, has had a lasting effect on her.

The significance of this event can't be overlooked. SGT Hester was the first female soldier since World War II to receive the Silver Star. However, she doesn't dwell on that fact. "It really doesn't have anything to do with being a female," she said. "It's about the duties I performed that day as a soldier."

"Without a word, this uniform also whispers of freezing troops, injured bodies, and Americans left forever in foreign fields. It documents every servicemen's courage who by accepting this uniform promises the one gift he truly has to give, his life. I wear my uniform for the heritage of sacrifice it represents and more. I wear my uniform with pride for it represents the greatest nation of free people in the world." ~ Capt. Karen Dorman Kimmele

We welcome hearing how this book has influenced the way you think, the way you lead, or the results you have achieved because of what you've learned in it. Please feel free to share your thoughts with us by email at:

mack@mackstory.com or bbriggs@eden-project.com

For information on Mack and Ria Story's other books and resources, please visit: www.TopStoryLeadership.com

For information on Bren Briggs and The Eden Project, please visit www.Eden-Project.com

Excerpt from

Defining Influence
by Mack Story

Note: In *Defining Influence*, I outline the foundational leadership principles and lessons we must learn in order to develop our character in a way that allows us to increase our influence with others. I also share many of my personal stories revealing how I got it wrong many times in the past and how I grew from front-line factory worker to become a Leadership Expert.

INTRODUCTION

"Leadership is influence. Nothing more. Nothing less. Everything rises and falls on leadership."
~ John C. Maxwell

Everyone is born a leader.

I haven't always believed everyone is a leader. You may or may not at this point. That's okay. There is a lot to learn about leadership.

At this very moment, you may already be thinking to yourself, "I'm not a leader." My goal is to help you understand why everyone is a leader and to help you develop a deeper understanding of the principles of leadership and influence.

Developing a deep understanding of leadership, has changed my life for the better. It has also changed the lives of my family members, friends, associates, and clients. I want to help you improve not only your life, but also the lives of those around you.

Until I became a student of leadership which eventually led me to become a John Maxwell Team Certified Leadership Coach, Trainer, and Speaker, and author, I did not understand leadership or realize everyone can benefit from learning the related principles.

In the past, I thought leadership was a term associated with being the boss and having formal authority over others. Those people are definitely leaders. But, I had been missing something. All of the other seven billion people on the planet are leaders too.

Why do I say everyone is born a leader? I agree with John Maxwell, "Leadership is Influence. Nothing more. Nothing less." Everyone has influence. It's a fact. Therefore, everyone is a leader.

No matter your age, gender, religion, race, nationality, location, or position, everyone has influence. Whether you want to be a leader or not, you are. After reading this book, I hope you do not question whether or not you are a leader. However, I do hope you question what type of leader you are and what level leader you are.

Everyone does not have authority, but everyone does have influence. There are plenty of examples in the world of people without authority leading people through influence alone. Actually, every one of us is an example. We have already done it. We know it is true. This principle is self-evident which means it contains its own evidence and does not need to be demonstrated or explained; it is obvious to everyone.

The question to ask is not, "Are you a leader?" The question is, "What type of leader are you?" The answer: Whatever kind you choose to be. Choosing not to be a leader is not an option. As long as you live, you will have influence. You are a leader.

You had influence before you were born and may have influence after your death. How? Thomas Edison still influences the world every time a light is turned on, you may do things in your life to influence others long after you're gone. Or, you may pass away with few people noticing. It depends on the choices you make.

Even when you're alone, you have influence. The most important person you will ever influence is yourself. The degree to which you influence yourself determines the level of influence you ultimately have with others. Typically, when we are talking about leading ourselves, the word most commonly used to describe self-leadership is discipline which can be defined as giving yourself a command and following through with it. We must practice discipline daily to increase our influence with others. It is not something we do only when we feel like it.

"We must all suffer one of two things: the pain of discipline or the pain of regret or disappointment."
~ Jim Rohn

As I define leadership as influence, keep in mind the word leadership and influence can be interchanged anytime and anyplace. They are one and the same. Throughout this book, I'll help you remember by placing one of the words in parentheses next to the other occasionally as a reminder. They are synonyms. When you read one, think of the other.

Everything rises and falls on influence (leadership). When you share what you're learning, clearly define leadership as influence for others. They need to understand the context of what you are teaching and understand they *are* leaders (people with influence) too. If you truly want to learn and apply leadership principles, you must start teaching this material to others within 24-48 hours of learning it yourself.

You will learn the foundational principles of leadership (influence) which will help you understand the importance of the following five questions. You will be able to take effective action by growing yourself and possibly others to a higher level of leadership (influence). Everything you ever achieve, internally and externally, will be a direct result of your influence.

1. **Why do we influence?** – Our character determines *why* we influence. Who we are on the inside is what matters. Do we manipulate or motivate? It's all about intent.

2. *How* do we influence? – Our character, combined with our competency, determines *how* we influence. Who we are and what we know combine to create our unique style of influence which determines our methods of influence.

3. *Where* do we influence? – Our passion and purpose determine *where* we have the greatest influence. What motivates and inspires us gives us the energy and authenticity to motivate and inspire others.

4. *Who* do we influence? – We influence those *who* buy-in to us. Only those valuing and seeking what we value and seek will volunteer to follow us. They give us or deny us permission to influence them based on how well we have developed our character and competency.

5. *When* do we influence? – We influence others *when* they want our influence. We choose when others influence us. Everyone else has the same choice. They decide when to accept or reject our influence. We only influence others when they want to change.

The first three questions are about the choices we make as we lead (influence) ourselves and others. The last two questions deal more with the choices others will make as they decide first, *if* they will follow us, and second, *when* they will follow us. They will base their choices on *who we are* and *what we know*.

Asking these questions is important. Knowing the answers is more important. But, taking action based on the answers is most important. Cumulatively, the answers to these questions determine our leadership style and our level of influence (leadership).

On a scale of 1-10, your influence can be very low level (1) to very high level (10). But make no mistake, you *are* a leader. You *are* always on the scale. The higher on the scale you are the more effective you are. You will be at different levels with different people at different times depending on many different variables.

Someone thinking they are not a leader or someone that doesn't want to be a leader, is still a leader. They will simply remain a low level leader with low level influence getting low level results. They will likely spend much time frustrated with many areas of their life. Although they could influence a change, they choose instead to be primarily influenced by others.

What separates higher level leaders from lower level leaders? There are many things, but two primary differences are:

1) Higher level leaders accept more responsibility in all areas of their lives while lower level leaders tend to blame others and transfer responsibility more often.

2) Higher level leaders have more positive influence while lower level leaders tend to have more negative influence.

My passion has led me to grow into my purpose which is to help others increase their influence personally and professionally while setting and reaching their goals. I am very passionate and have great conviction. I have realized many benefits by getting better results in all areas of my life. I have improved relationships with my family members, my friends, my associates, my peers, and my clients. I have witnessed people within these same groups embrace leadership principles and reap the same benefits.

The degree to which I *live* what I teach determines my effectiveness. My goal is to learn it, live it, and *then* teach it. I had major internal struggles as I grew my way to where I am. I'm a long way from perfect, so I seek daily improvement. Too often, I see people teaching leadership but not living what they're teaching. If I teach it, I apply it.

My goal is to be a better leader tomorrow than I am today. I simply have to get out of my own way and lead. I must lead me effectively before I can lead others effectively, not only with acquired knowledge, but also with experience from applying and living the principles.

I'll be transparent with personal stories to help you see how I have applied leadership principles by sharing: How I've struggled. How I've learned. How I've sacrificed. How I've succeeded.

Go beyond highlighting or underlining key points. Take the time to write down your thoughts related to the principle. Write down what you want to change. Write down how you can apply the principle in your life. You may want to consider getting a journal to fully capture your thoughts as you progress through the chapters. What you are thinking as you read is often much more important than what you're reading.

Most importantly, do not focus your thoughts on others. Yes, they need it too. We all need it. I need it. You need it. If you focus outside of yourself, you are missing the very point. Your influence comes from within. Your influence rises and falls based on your choices. You have untapped and unlimited potential waiting to be released. Only you can release it.

You, like everyone else, were born a leader. Let's take a leadership journey together.

Note: If you enjoyed this Introduction to *Defining Influence*, it is available in paperback and as an eBook on Amazon.com or for a signed paperback copy you can purchase at www.TopStoryLeadership.com.

Note: For additional free downloads visit:
www.MackStory.com
and
www.Blue-CollarLeadership.com

Excerpt from

10 Values of High Impact Leaders
by Mack Story

Our values are the foundation upon which we build our character. I'll be sharing 10 values high impact leaders work to master because they know these values will have a tremendous impact on their ability to lead others well. You may be thinking, "Aren't there more than 10 leadership values?" Absolutely! They seem to be endless. And, they are all important. These are simply 10 values I believe are key.

Since leadership is very dynamic, the more values you have been able to internalize and utilize synergistically together, the more effective you will be. The more influence you will have.

"High performing organizations that continuously invest in leadership development are now defining new 21st century leadership models to deal with today's gaps in their leadership pipelines and the new global business environment. These people-focused organizations have generated nearly 60% improved business growth, reported a 66% improvement in bench strength, and showed a 62% improvement in employee retention. And, our research shows that it is not enough to just spend money on leadership training, but rather to follow specific practices that drive accelerated business results." ~ Josh Bersin

Do you want to be a high impact leader?

I believe everyone is a leader, but they are leading at different levels.
I believe everyone can and should lead from *where they are.*

I believe everyone can and should make a high impact.
I believe growth doesn't just happen; we must make it happen.
I believe before you will invest in yourself you must first believe in yourself.
I believe leaders must believe in their team before they will invest in their team.
I truly believe *everything rises and falls on influence.*

There is a story of a tourist who paused for a rest in a small town in the mountains. He went over to an old man sitting on a bench in front of the only store in town and inquired, "Friend, can you tell me something this town is noted for?"

"Well," replied the old man, "I don't rightly know except it's the starting point to the world. You can start here and go anywhere you want."

That's a great little story. We are all at "the starting point" to the world, and we "can start here and go anywhere we want." We can expand our influence 360° in all directions by starting in the center with ourselves.

Consider the following illustration. Imagine you are standing in the center. You can make a high impact. However, it will not happen by accident. You must become intentional. You must live with purpose while focusing on your performance as you develop your potential.

Note: Illustration and The 10 Values are listed on the following pages.

Why we do what we do is about our *purpose*.

How we do what we do is about our *performance*.

What we do will determine our *potential*.

Where these three components overlap, you will achieve a **HIGH IMPACT**.

The 10 Values of High Impact Leaders

1
THE VALUE OF VISION
Vision is the foundation of hope.
"When there's hope in the future, there's power in the present." ~ Les Brown

2
THE VALUE OF MODELING
Someone is always watching you.
"Who we are on the inside is what people see on the outside." ~ Mack Story

3
THE VALUE OF RESPONSIBILITY
When we take responsibility, we take control.
"What is common sense is not always common practice." ~ Dr. Stephen R. Covey

4
THE VALUE OF TIMING
It matters when you do what you do.
"It's about doing the right thing for the right reason at the right time." ~ Mack Story

5
THE VALUE OF RESPECT
To be respected, we must be respectful.
"Go See, ask why, and show respect."
~ Jim Womack

6
THE VALUE OF EMPOWERMENT
Leaders gain influence by
giving it to others.
"Leadership is not reserved for leaders."
~ Marcus Buckingham

7
THE VALUE OF DELEGATION
We should lead with questions
instead of directions.
"Delegation 101: Delegating 'what to do,' makes you responsible. Delegating 'what to accomplish,' allows others to become responsible." ~ Mack Story

8
THE VALUE OF MULTIPLICATION
None of us is as influential as all of us.
"To add growth, lead followers. To multiply, lead leaders." ~ John C. Maxwell

9
THE VALUE OF RESULTS
Leaders like to make things happen.
"Most people fail in the getting started."
~ Maureen Falcone

10
THE VALUE OF SIGNIFICANCE
Are you going to settle for success?
"Significance is a choice that only successful people can make."
~ Mack Story

ABOUT MACK STORY

Mack's story is an amazing journey of personal and professional growth. He married Ria in 2001. He has one son, Eric, born in 1991.

After graduating from high school in 1987, Mack joined the United States Marine Corps Reserve as a 0311 infantryman. Soon after in 1988, he began his career in manufacturing on the front lines of a production machine shop. Graduating with highest honors, he earned an Executive Bachelor of Business Administration degree from Faulkner University in 2002.

Mack began his career in manufacturing on the front lines of a machine shop. He grew himself into upper management and found his niche in lean manufacturing and along with it, developed his passion for leadership. He has logged more than 11,000 hours leading leaders and their cross-functional teams through various types of organizational change and transformation. He understands everything rises and falls on influence.

In 2008, he launched *KaizenOps*, a Lean Manufacturing and Leadership Development firm, which operates today as *Top Story Leadership*, offering professional leadership speaking, training, and coaching/mentoring.

Mack is a John C. Maxwell Certified Leadership Coach, Trainer, and Speaker. His experience with John includes an international training event as part of the Cultural Transformation in Guatemala where over 20,000 leaders were trained in one week.

Mack has also been trained by, and shared the stage with, internationally recognized motivational speaker Les Brown.

Mack is also the author of other books: *Blue-Collar Leadership*, *Blue-Collar Leadership & Supervision*, *Defining Influence*, *10 Values of High Impact Leaders*, and *Change Happens*.

Mack is an inspiration for people everywhere as an example of achievement, growth, and personal development. His passion motivates and inspires people all over the world!

ABOUT BREN BRIGGS

Bren is a retired Army officer with 28 years of distinguished service. He has multiple awards and accommodations including two meritorious service medals.

Bren graduated from Troy State University in Dothan, AL with a BA in Sociology and later earned an MA from Shorter University in Leadership.

Bren served at multiple levels of leadership throughout his career to include company command and multiple operations positions. Bren served as a medical operations officer on two counter terrorism teams, was the acquisition officer during one of his deployments, and finished his career at the Army Reserve Headquarters as the senior Lean Six Sigma Master Black Belt for the Army Reserve.

Bren is the Founder and Executive Director of *The Eden Project*, a warrior support foundation created to help warriors and their families reunite after long separations, deployments, and specifically to heal and cope with battle injuries.

The Eden Project supports and provides tools for family reunification, healing, warrior to civilian training, and provides a holistic approach to medical healing.

The core objective of *The Eden Project* is to focus on what Bren calls R-4 by helping:

- Restore marriages
- Rebuild bodies
- Rejuvenate minds
- Restart futures

TOP STORY LEADERSHIP

Leadership Development & Lean Manufacturing Support

- ✓ Keynote Speaking – conferences & seminars
- ✓ On-site Corporate Training: includes Mack's own fully customized material and Learning Systems based on some of John C. Maxwell's best-selling books
- ✓ On-site Half-day/Full-day Workshops/Seminars
- ✓ Power of Effective Planning Program
- ✓ Power of Effective Communication Program
- ✓ Change Happens Program
- ✓ LDRSHP Boot Camp Program
- ✓ High Impact Leadership Program
- ✓ Individual and Team Coaching
- ✓ Individual and Team Mentoring
- ✓ Corporate Retreats
- ✓ Partnership Summits
- ✓ On-site Lean Leadership Certification
- ✓ On-site Lean Manufacturing Certification
- ✓ On-site Lean Manufacturing Event Facilitation
- ✓ On-site Lean Manufacturing Training

For more information please visit:

www.TopStoryLeadership.com

www.linkedin.com/in/mackstory

www.facebook.com/mack.story

www.Blue-CollarLeadership.com

www.Eden-Project.com

Order Mack's other books online from Amazon or his website: www.TopStoryLeadership.com

High Impact leaders align their habits with key values in order to maximize their influence. High impact leaders intentionally grow and develop themselves in an effort to more effectively grow and develop others.

These 10 Values are commonly understood. However, they are not always commonly practiced. These 10 values will help you build trust and accelerate relationship building. Those mastering these 10 values will be able to lead with speed as they develop 360° of influence from wherever they are.

Order Mack's other books online from Amazon or his website: www.TopStoryLeadership.com

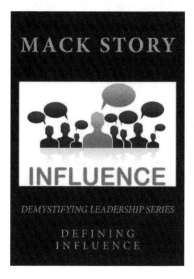

Are you looking for transformation in your life? Do you want better results? Do you want stronger relationships?

In *Defining Influence*, Mack breaks down many of the principles that will allow anyone at any level to methodically and intentionally increase their positive influence.

Mack blends his personal growth journey with lessons on the principles he learned along the way. He's not telling you what he learned after years of research, but rather what he learned from years of application and transformation. Everything rises and falls on influence.

Order Mack's other books online from Amazon or his website:
www.TopStoryLeadership.com

"I wish someone had given me this book 30 years ago when I started my career on the front lines. It would have changed my life then. It can change your life now." ~ Mack Story

Separate yourself from the crowd quickly by learning how to master the traits High Impact leaders value most. You will learn how to get noticed by high impact leaders and how to get promoted for the right reasons. You will learn how to become recognized as a front line leader worth following, and you don't need formal authority (position) because you will develop something better: moral authority (influence).

**Down load the first 5 chapters now at:
www.Blue-CollarLeadership.com**

Order Mack's other books online from Amazon or his website: www.TopStoryLeadership.com

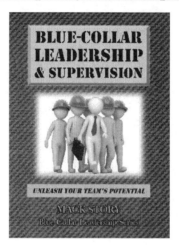

High impact leadership starts with you but it's not about you. Who you are will determine how you lead. High impact leaders lead on purpose. *Blue-Collar Leadership & Supervision* offers you a simple, easy to understand explanation of foundational leadership principles that you can apply immediately to improve your results. This is "Leadership 101" for leaders of those on the front lines.

You will learn how to become a leader worth following, how to make a bigger impact, and most importantly, how to unleash your team's potential. This is be perfect resource for anyone already leading those on the front lines or those on the front lines who want to work their way into a leadership position.

www.BlueCollarLeaders.com

Order Ria's other books online from Amazon or her website: www.TopStoryLeadership.com

Ria's Story: From Ashes to Beauty is the unforgettable story and inspirational memoir of a young woman who was sexually abused by her father, and then, rejected by her mother. Determined to not only survive, but to also thrive, Ria shares how she was able to overcome the odds and find hope and healing to Achieve Abundant Life. She shares leadership principles she applied to find professional success and personal significance, and how she was able to find the courage to share her story to give hope to others around the world.

Order Ria's other books online from Amazon or her website: www.TopStoryLeadership.com

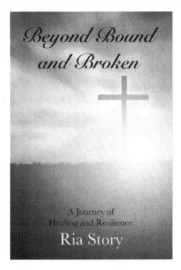

What does it mean to be resilient? We all face adversity in life. The question is, "How will you respond to it?" Will you learn to be resilient? Will you learn to thrive or merely survive?

Ria shares how she overcame shame, fear, and doubt that stemmed from seven years of sexually abuse by her father and others. She is a COURAGE WARRIOR.

By experiencing Ria's journey of healing and resilience, you will find courage for your own. What happens to us in life isn't as important as how we respond to what happens. The choices we make today will define us tomorrow.

Order Ria's other books online from Amazon or her website: www.TopStoryLeadership.com

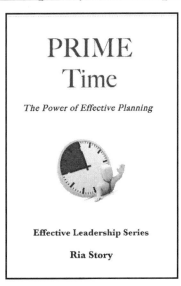

Are you living your life in PRIME Time? Are you living and working in alignment with your purpose, passion and personal mission? Are you living an abundant life, accomplishing your goals, and achieving your dreams?

In *PRIME Time: The Power of Effective Planning*, you will learn how to set and achieve the goals that are important to you, how to set boundaries, and how to increase effectiveness at home and at work. Complete with personal coaching worksheets, you will walk step-by-step through your individual action plan to achieve success and harmony in each of the four dimensions of life: physical, mental, relational, and spiritual.

Order Ria's other books online from Amazon or her website: www.TopStoryLeadership.com

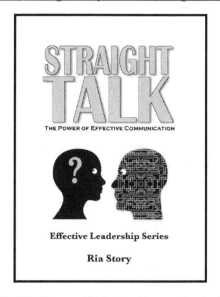

Straight Talk: The Power of Effective Communication is the third book in Ria's Effective Leadership Series. It's packed full of principles that will help you make an impact through effective communication.

In *Straight Talk*, Ria shares tools on how to become a better communicator, how to become a more effective connector, and how improving those skills will help you increase your influence in every situation. When you're able to increase your influence, you're well on your way to increasing your options. Everything rises and falls on influence.

Order Mack and Ria's other books online from Amazon or their website:
www.TopStoryLeadership.com

Are you leveraging change to create opportunities for yourself? If not, you're getting left behind by those who are. Learn to leverage change to increase your influence.

In this book, you will learn how to make change your friend and not your enemy. You will learn the value of embracing change, supporting change, leveraging change, initiating change, and ultimately leading change. And also, why none of it matters unless you have the courage to change. When you increase your influence, you increase your options.

Made in the USA
Charleston, SC
30 August 2016